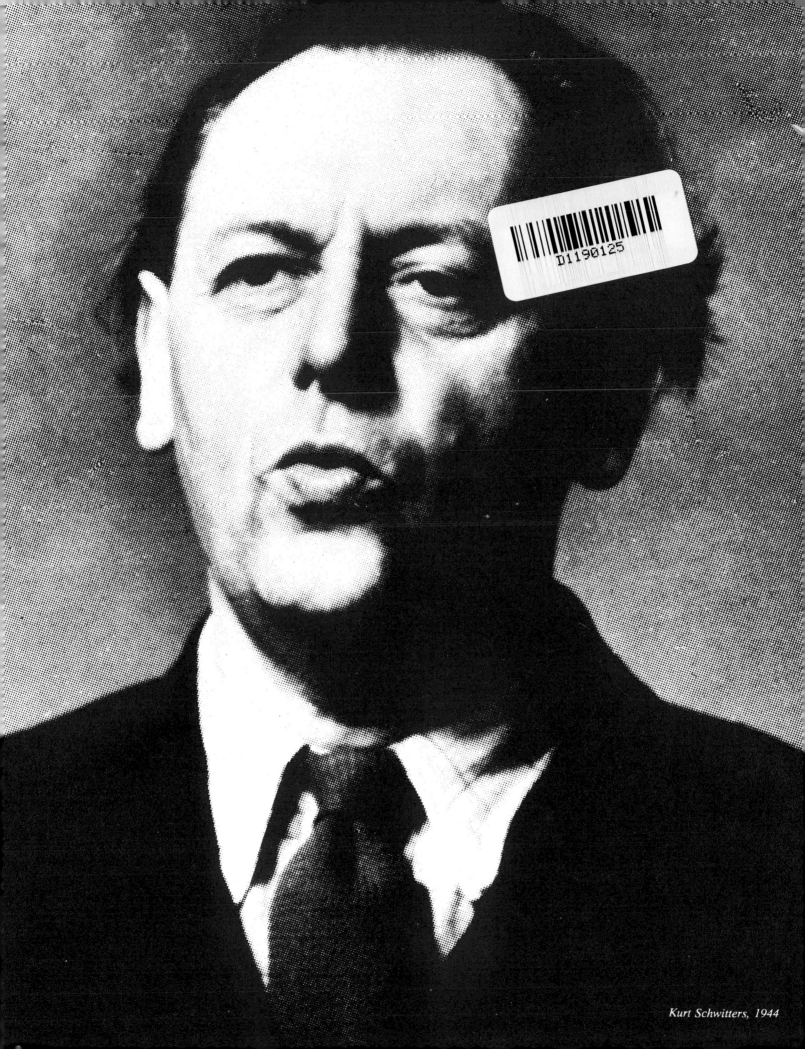

Kurt Schwitters, 1944

Also by Jackson Mac Low

The Twin Plays: Port-Au-Prince & Adams County Illinois
(Mac Low & Bloedow, 1963; 2nd ed., Something Else, 1966)

The Pronouns--A Collection of 40 Dances--For the Dancers
(Mac Low & Judson Dance Workshop, 1964; 2nd ed., Tetrad, 1971; 3rd ed., Station Hill, 1979)

Verdurous Sanguinaria [play] (Southern University, 1967)

August Light Poems (Caterpillar Books, 1967)

22 Light Poems (Black Sparrow, 1968)

23rd Light Poem: For Larry Eigner (Tetrad, 1969)

Stanzas for Iris Lezak (Something Else, 1972)

4 trains (Burning Deck, 1974)

36th Light Poem: In Memoriam Buster Keaton (Permanent Press, 1975)

21 Matched Asymmetries (Aloes Books, 1978)

54th Light Poem: For Ian Tyson (Membrane, 1978)

A Dozen Douzains for Eve Rosenthal (Gronk Books, 1978)

phone (Printed Editions and Kontexts, 1978)

Asymmetries 1-260 (Printed Editions, 1980)

"Is That Wool Hat My Hat?" (Membrane, 1982)

From Pearl Harbor Day to FDR's Birthday (Sun & Moon, 1982)

Bloomsday (Station Hill, 1984)

French Sonnets (Black Mesa, 1984; 2nd ed., Membrane, 1989)

The Virginia Woolf Poems (Burning Deck, 1985)

Eight Drawing-Asymmetries [boxed serigraphs] (Francesco Conz, 1985)

Representative Works: 1938-1985 (Roof Books, 1986)

Words nd Ends from Ez (Avenue B, 1989)

Twenties: 100 Poems (Roof Books, 1991)

Pieces o' Six: Thirty-three Poems in Prose (Sun & Moon, 1992)

42 Merzgedichte in Memoriam *Kurt Schwitters*

(FEBRUARY 1987 – SEPTEMBER 1989)

Jackson Mac Low

"The facts of life are not especially interesting to write about:
one can't lie, one hasn't experienced anything significant,
and yet one lives."
Kurt Schwitters

STATION HILL

First Edition.

Published by Station Hill Literary Editions under the Institute for Publishing Arts, Inc., Barrytown, New York 12507, with grateful acknowledgement to the National Endowment for the Arts, a federal agency in Washington, D.C., and the New York State Council on the Arts, for partial financial support of this project.

"Merzgedichte 1" (Pieces o'Six-32) is reprinted by permission of the publisher from *Pieces o'Six:Thirty-Three Poems in Prose (1983-1987)* (Los Angeles: Sun & Moon, 1992), pages 11-13.

Front cover art: the painting "MERZ VORTRAGSABEND" copyright © 1990 by Anne Tardos. Photographs of Jackson Mac Low on back cover copyright © 1992 and on page 230 copyright © 1993 by Anne Tardos.

Cover designed by Susan Quasha, with painting and photograph by Anne Tardos.
Text designed by Jackson Mac Low.

Library of Congress Cataloging-in-Publication Data

Mac Low, Jackson
    42 Merzgedichte in memoriam Kurt Schwitters : (February
1987-September 1989) / Jackson Mac Low.
        p.   cm.
    ISBN 0-88268-145-1 : $14.95
    1. Schwitters, Kurt, 1887-1948—Poetry. 2. Visual poetry,
American. I. Schwitters, Kurt, 1887-1948. II. Title. III. Title:
Forty-two Merzgedichte in memoriam Kurt Schwitters.
PS3563.A228A615 1994
811'.54—dc20   94-5275
                                                  CIP

Manufactured in the United States of America.

Contents

Introduction

Kurt Schwitters (1887-1948) was an incredibly productive and inventive visual, literary, and performance artist. He worked as a collagist, painter, sculptor, and maker of what have since become known as assemblages, combines, and installations (notably, his *Merzbauten*, the largest of which, in Hanover (destroyed during World War II), came to occupy most of a building's interior, and in making which he also functioned as an architect), as well as a typographer and designer. He also wrote innumerable poems, stories, plays, and unclassifiable verbal works of art, including some of the first examples of what is now called sound poetry and text-sound texts, which he performed magnificently. While some of his contemporaries called their work and themselves "Dada," he adopted the syllable "*MERZ*" from a snippet of an advertisement for a commercial and private bank (*Commerz- und Privatbank*) that he glued to a collage, applying it not only to that collage (*Das Merzbild*), but eventually to all his artwork--and ultimately to himself.

When I first became acquainted with his collages and poems, in the early 1940s, my spontaneous response was a feeling of pleasure, love, and kinship. This feeling has grown steadily as I have come to know more and more of his work in all fields. So when Michael Erlhoff and Klaus Stadtmüller invited me in January 1987 to contribute to their *Kurt Schwitters Almanach 1987* (Hannover: Postskriptum Verlag), which they planned as an "hommage" in honor of the centennial of his birth in June 1887, I was delighted to accept their invitation.

At that time I was writing a series of poems in prose called *Pieces o' Six* (Los Angeles: Sun & Moon, 1992). The title came from the fact that the first one occupied exactly six handwritten pages in a 200 page notebook. I decided to fill that notebook with such pieces, so that the series would ultimately include 33 six-page poems in prose (198 divided by 6, with a remainder of two notebook pages for front or back matter). However, as I continued the series, I found myself making revisions when typing them, so the "six" came to refer to the number of pages in the handwritten *first draft* of each one. Then soon after I began writing on computers, early in 1987, I completed the first draft of "Pieces o' Six -- XXXI" (whose first sentence had been written in the Louvre in July 1986): the "six" became the number of *computer* pages in the first draft.

Thus it was that I began writing an "hommage" to Schwitters on my computer as "Pieces o' Six -- XXXII," and because of its subject and dedicatee, I decided to take advantage of the typographical possibilities (e.g., changes of character format corresponding to changes of "voice") offered by the computer (limited as they were at the time by the capabilities of my word processor and my dot-matrix printer). I also adopted a collage method involving "impulse-chance" appropriations, adaptations, paraphrases, etc., mainly from two books lent me by the poet, essayist, and psychoanalyst Nick Piombino: Werner Schmalenbach's *Kurt Schwitters* (Cologne: Verlag M. DuMont Schauberg, 1967; English version, New York: Harry N. Abrams, 1977) and John Elderfield's *Kurt Schwitters* (London and New York: Thames and Hudson, 1985).

I call the method used in writing "Pieces o' Six -- XXXII" *impulse chance* because I found the various words, phrases, sentences, etc. (mainly from Schwitters and his contemporaries, notably Tristan Tzara and Richard Huelsenbeck, and the authors of the two sources) by flipping rapidly through the source books and taking into my text whatever spontaneously appealed to me, though often modifying, excerpting, or paraphrasing the sources. Occasionally I interpolated sentences of my own.

I called "Pieces o' Six -- XXXII" a *Merzgedicht* [MERZ poem] in Memoriam *Kurt Schwitters*" because of both its subject matter and its collage-like structure. However, when I wrote it, I had no idea that it was the first of a *series* of *Merzgedichte*. But soon after I finished it, I devised a chance-operational method that used random digits (generated by a simple Turbo-C program) and the "glossary" capabilities of my word processor, Microsoft Word, to select certain linguistic units from "Pieces o' Six -- XXXII" and to juxtapose them and place them on the pages in entirely new constellations. When I completed the first poem produced by this method, the "*2nd Merzgedicht* in Memoriam *Kurt Schwitters*," I realized that a *new* series of poems had sprouted from the "Pieces o' Six" (like a new bough branching from an older one near its end).

I continued writing the series intermittently from March 1987 to September 1989, often modifying the compositional methods (thus producing many different kinds of texts) and from time to time adding new linguistic units from the sources to my glossary lists. Later, certain verbal elements in one glossary unaccountably became fragmented and/or "jammed together" when I added too many entries--an accident gleefully accepted and turned to use. However, while the spacing of the elements on the pages was originally determined by chance operations, it was modified in part when I changed from the dot-matrix printer to a laser printer and from a type font with equal spacing to one with proportional spacing. Rather than using chance operations to respace everything written up to that point, I more or less imitated the look of the dot-matrix printouts, but sometimes I consciously "edited" their spacing even more. I had to do this again in the course of preparing the printouts from which the present edition was reproduced: among other things, I had to augment the amount of space between the lines of type and to widen the margins.

In addition, around Bloomsday (June 16) 1989, Charles O. Hartman, a poet, critic, and professor (at Connecticut College in New London), sent me his computer program DIASTEXT, his first automation of one of the "diastic" text-selection and composition procedures that I had developed in January 1963 and had been using intermittently ever since.

When I use a diastic procedure, I read through a source text and take into my text various linguistic units, ranging from single words (*The Virginia Woolf Poems*, Providence: Burning Deck, 1985), or even parts of words (*Words nd Ends from Ez*, Bolinas: Avenue B, 1989), to phrases, larger sentence fragments, and whole sentences, in which the letters of an "index" text appear in the letter and word strings drawn from the source text in places *corresponding to* those they occupy in the "index." E.g., using the word "poet" from the first sentence of the previous paragraph as "index" and the rest of that and the present paragraph as source, appropriating only single words, using capitals and punctuation marks to begin and end lines, and doing no editing, I would produce the following text (the letters, utilized four times, are set in boldface):

program composition been text
Poems words,
Avenue text **p**laces *corresponding* they
"**p**oet"
previous source,
the text

DIASTEXT uses the *whole source text* as the "index"; a later version, DIASTEX4, sent to me in August 1989, allows the user to choose and employ a separate index text.

Prof. Hartman also sent me the latest version of TRAVESTY, a program that generates "pseudo-texts," written by the critic Hugh Kenner and the computer scientist Joseph O'Rourke and first published in *BYTE* magazine in November 1984. In their words, TRAVESTY uses "English letter-combination frequencies . . . to generate random text that mimics the frequencies found in a sample. Though nonsensical, these pseudo-texts have a haunting plausibility, preserving as they do many recognizable mannerisms of the texts from which they are derived. . . . *[F]or an order-n scan, every n-character sequence in the output occurs somewhere in the input, and at about the same frequency.*" According to what "order" of "travesty" one chooses to generate, one may generate either texts that seem fairly close to normal English or ones that are far from it.

I utilized these programs in different ways, employing earlier *Merzgedichte* as source texts: (1) For the *31st Merzgedicht*, I ran the *25th Merzgedicht* through DIASTEXT alone. (2) For the *32nd*, I ran the *4th* through DIASTEXT alone. (3) For the *33rd*, I ran the *2nd* through DIASTEX4 alone. (4) For the *34th*, I ran the *8th* through DIASTEX4 alone. (5) For the *35th*, I ran the *9th* through DIASTEX4 alone. (6) And for the *36th* through the *42nd*, I ran the *29th* first through TRAVESTY, asking for "low-order" output--i.e., scanning for sequences of very few characters, to insure the outputting predominantly of letter strings that aren't real words (pseudo-words), along with a few real words, most of them embedded in pseudo-words--and then through DIASTEX4. I also submitted the output, in most cases, to certain systematic types of postediting, mainly of format and capitalization, some of which amounted to final chance operations.

(Hartman and Kenner have written the book *Sentences*, forthcoming from Sun & Moon, Los Angeles, "by running the text of *Sentences for Analysis and Parsing from the Thayer Street Grammar School* [Providence, R.I., presumably mid-19th century] through TRAVESTY many times [asking for moderately "high-order" output], selecting appealing outputs, and running those through DIASTEXT," as Hartman wrote me.)

The *42 Merzgedichte* in Memoriam *Kurt Schwitters*, like their dedicatee and his works, are "polymedial": they share the characteristics of several arts. They are poems--literary artworks--in various formats: prose, verse, and ones sharing characteristics of both. The verbal elements in most of them are meaningful in the usual sense of the word and directly related to the artist to whose memory they are dedicated. And like those of most of his works, these elements are placed abruptly next to each other as images, color areas, and objects are placed in visual collages and assemblages, so the *Merzgedichte* are works of collage art.

They are also musical compositions in that words, phrases, sentences, and other linguistic elements are treated like the tones or intervals of scales or of tone rows, melodic themes or motifs, or rhythmic figures, recurring again and again (in full or fragmentarily) in various combinations and concatenations. (In this regard they resemble several earlier works of mine, notably *The Pronouns*, in which a gamut of action predicates is treated similarly.) Moreover, the *22nd Merzgedicht* includes both a performance text, musical notation, and performance instructions (which appear at the end of this book), and many of the other *Merzgedichte* may best be appreciated through live or recorded performances rather than solely by silent reading.

This is especially true of the last group (the *36th* through the *42nd Merzgedichte*), produced by recycling earlier ones through low-order TRAVESTY scannings and DIASTEX4, which are clearly "text-sound texts."

I have performed "low-order travesties" with Anne Tardos at a number of places here and abroad, notably at the arts festival Milanopoesia (Milan, 24 September 1989); during the S.E.M. Ensemble program "Spoken Music" (Paula Cooper Gallery, New York, 6 January 1990), of which a cassette recording is available from the S.E.M. Ensemble, P.O. Box 37, Brooklyn, NY 11215; and at the Schule für Dichtung in Wien (Kursalon Hübner, Vienna, 10 April 1992) This Vienna performance, in which Anne and I perform the *38th* and *39th Merzgedichte* simultaneously, is included on XI 110, a compact disc of some of my music and performance works released in 1993 by Experimental Intermedia (224 Centre St., New York, NY 10013).

Finally, the way the *Merzgedichte* look on their pages is as important as their verbal elements (*including their meanings*) and their verbal-musical organization, so they are clearly works of visual art as well as poems, collages, musical compositions, and performance texts.

For her manifold support during the writing of this book and for her invaluable help during the preparation and checking of the printouts that were the camera copy for its printing, I wish to thank my wife, Anne Tardos.

AD MAIOREM MERZI GLORIAM

Jackson Mac Low
16 - 18 August 1990 and 19 - 23 February 1993
New York

1st Merzgedicht in Memoriam *Kurt Schwitters*

First word for Kurt Schwitters: *Merz*. **If I ever move from Hannover, where I love and hate everything, I will lose the feeling that makes my *world point of view*.** 1887. **Now I call myself** MERZ. A *degenerate artist. Merzbilde med regnbue. Entformung, Eigengift, konsequent, Urbegriff.* This was before H.R.H. The Late Duke of Clarence & Avondale. Now it is a Merzpicture. Sorry! Average Merz-drawings: 4 to 8 inches high; some very large collages: 11 to 14 inches high, occasionally 15 to 24 inches high; but many *Aphorismer* less than 4 inches high. Never believed he was making anything but pure abstract forms. Selected discarded unfinished pages from Molling's Hannover printing shop and rode off on his bicycle with as many as he could carry. Through *Entformung* he attempted to clean away the *Eigengift* to gather them into the paradise of art's *Urbegriff.* **The picture is a self-contained work of art.** *Merz ist form.* **It refers to nothing outside itself.** ART NEEDS CONTEMPLATIVE SELF-ABSORPTION. Schwitters was fascinated with printed matter and regarded words and letters both as meaningful symbols and as formal design elements. **A consistent work of art can never refer to anything outside itself without loosening its ties to art.** One's first glimpses of Schwitters in the 1940s: possibly in Chicago, probably in New York. A r t i s a u t o n o m o u s . *Auch in der Malerei verwende ich für die Komposition gern die Brocken des täglichen Abfalls etwa wie der Schacko aufgebaut ist aus den Reden seiner Besitzerin.* NEVER DO WHAT ANYONE ELSE HAS DONE. ALWAYS DO OTHERWISE THAN THE OTHERS. **I have Merzed banalities.** In 1924 he set up an advertising agency in Hannover and designed ads, notably for Pelikan ink, from one of which an *elikan* survives in a 1925 Merz. Mz 1926, 12. reclining emm. Schwitters had no concern for desanctification. *Schnuppe / meine süsse puppe, / mir ist alles schnuppe, / wenn ich meine schnauze / auf die deine bautze.* Schwitters gradually dropped avant-garde devices from his writing in the later 1920s and wrote in more nearly conventional styles (needless to say, the resultant works were hardly conventional). Schacko was a parrot who pulled out all his feathers except those on the top of his head because he couldn't sleep since the dying father kept the lights on all night because he was in such pain *he* couldn't sleep. Schwitters never pretended he didn't care about art. *Brutally Merzed wood reliefs and delicately articulated wooden constructions.* Huelsenbeck and Tzara, who agreed on little else, both saw him as a *petit bourgeois.* KommERZ *und Privatbank.* Some Dadaists trumpeted opposition to art while busily building artistic careers with Dadaism as an advertising device. WHEN WAS HIS WENN HANNOVERED FOR THE EIGENGIFT OF MALEREI? *Schwitters as I saw him was a man who ran away from reality.* He deeply valued art but took it very lightly. *MERZ-PICTURES ARE ABSTRACT WORKS OF ART.* Black Dots and Quadrangle. *If one reads Hannover backwards, one gets the* *combination* re von nah. *The word* re *one can read indifferently as **backward** or **back**. I suggest **backward**. Thus the translation of the word **Hannover** read backward would be **backward from near**. And that is correct, for then the translation of the word **Hannover** read forward would be **forward to far**. This means Hannover strives forward, even to infinity.* SCHWITTERS SHIED AWAY FROM LAYING BARE A **NEW REALITY** AND FROM ANTIARTISTIC GESTURES, RETAINING EVEN IN THE i-DRAWINGS A TRADITIONAL UNDERSTANDING OF ART: IN THE CASE OF i, THE ACT OF THE ARTIST IS SOLELY THE DISASSOCIATION [*ENTFORMELUNG*] OF A GIVEN OBJECT THROUGH SINGLING OUT A PART RHYTHMIC IN ITSELF. *Chanson des autres is i.* **Art as simple as writing the letter** i. *The middle vowel of the alphabet.* Schwitters taught us we can use anything to make art and even unaltered found materials may become art but the intention enacted in this praxis need include no antiartistic admixture. J 20 i-Zeichnung. *Go out into the whole world and make the truth known, the only truth there is, the truth about Anna Blume.* Had Schwitters lived to see FLUXUS, he'd have either scorned or scoffed at Maciunas's supposedly antiartistic tenets. Mz 1926, 9. with violet velvet. In a passage Schwitters underlined, Bluemner wrote that **Poetry is word composition** that **need not be in accord with logic and grammar** using a language that **at times sees itself reaching the end of all intensifications and possibilities of selection so that it is compelled to go back to its origins**. *Mz 410 something or other. Frühe rundet Regen blau.* THE MOST INTERNATIONAL PETIT BOURGEOIS IN THE WORLD. HIS DAILY LIFE WAS ENTIRELY WITHOUT BOURGEOIS COMFORTS. *A non-paying spectator on the Dadaist scene, by his very nature he was Dada.* Disjointed Forces. SCHWITTERS STOOD OUT among the Dadaists AS A MARVELOUS DILETTANTE. Today's *artist certifiers* would call him *a very persistent amateur. TYLL EULENSPIEGEL.* He'd have trouble being certified for an artist's loft in Soho. *Merz 14/15. Die Scheuche.* He lived in ONE OF THE LIVELIEST CITIES IN POSTWAR GERMANY *like a lower middle class Victorian.* **The Kaspar David Friedrich of the Dadaist revolution.** *He simply did not have a conventional bone in his body.* WHAT WAS ONCE CRIED DOWN AS MADNESS OR A BAD JOKE TURNS INTO A SOLID CULTURAL POSSESSION, AND THE REVOLUTIONARIES OF YESTERDAY ARE THE CLASSICS OF TODAY. That's just what the revolutionaries of today must avoid: becoming the classics of tomorrow! *Merz is as tolerant as possible with respect to its material.* Schwitters and Wordsworth lived their last years, died, and are buried--4 miles from each other--in England's Lake District. *MY BASIC TRAIT IS MELANCHOLY.* Schwitters died in June 1948. *Merzzeichnung 83 Zeichnung F.* Why make artworks if you're opposed to art? *My wet nurse's milk was too thick and there was too little, because she nursed me beyond the lawfully allowed time.* Playing Card Harmonica. *The materials bring into the abstract formal performance a piece of familiar reality.* Schwitters had a little garden in Isernhagen, a village near Hannover: *Roses, strawberries, a man-made hill, and an artificial pond. In the fall of 1901, village boys tore up the garden while I looked on. The excitement brought on St. Vitus's dance. I was sick for two years, totally disabled. Das Merzbild.* ELIKAN MERZED A KONSEQUENT BROCKEN. He loved each discarded bit or snippet for itself though he made it take its place in what he would have called an abstract structure. *Striving for expression in a* *work of art seems to me injurious to art.* <u>Mz 280 Red Pen (for Lisker).</u> He cared nothing about contradicting himself even though he thought that artworks had to be *konsequent.* ONE CAN EVEN SHOUT OUT THROUGH REFUSE, AND THIS IS WHAT I DID, NAILING AND GLUING IT TOGETHER. I CALLED IT MERZ, IT WAS A PRAYER ABOUT THE VICTORIOUS END OF THE WAR, VICTORIOUS AS ONCE AGAIN PEACE HAD WON IN THE END; EVERYTHING HAD BROKEN DOWN IN ANY CASE AND NEW THINGS HAD TO BE MADE OUT OF FRAGMENTS: AND THIS IS MERZ. IT WAS LIKE AN IMAGE OF THE REVOLUTION WITHIN ME, NOT AS IT WAS BUT AS IT SHOULD HAVE BEEN. <u>Construction for Noble Ladies.</u> *Such political convictions as he had were more against than for--against war, against the stupidity of institutions, programs, phrasemaking of every kind.* People such as Huelsenbeck (and even Schwitters himself) thought him nonpolitical because he espoused no easily recognized ideology, not realizing that Schwitters' artworks function politically by making the viewer look at the most banal detritus with (as poor Maciunas would have put it) *an art attitude,* which by distancing the objects of everyday experience allows her to see them in a strange context and from a new angle, so that whatever has been taken for granted may begin to be questioned and eventually illumined by critical reflection. *The increasing formalization of Schwitters' collages and relief assemblages in the early 1920s necessarily inhibited the more fantastic side of his artistic personality.* <u>Siegbild (Victory Picture), c. 1925.</u> Schwitters was hardly ever a pure image maker, unlike most Dada artists, who transmitted Dada's revolutionary message mainly through image-content. *Dada was ideological without a specific ideology and purposive without a purpose, which is why Dada actions and objects could be considered* artistic. FAUVIST COLOR WITHIN A CUBIST SYSTEM. <u>*Mz 387. Kaltensundheim, 1922*</u>: Merzed the year *this* Merzer was born. *Schwitters' method is that of Realism made from real things.* This is a **positive** link with FLUXUS--this kind of Realism is much more important to most so-called FLUXUS artists than the anti-art component, which Maciunas himself seems largely to have discounted before his untimely death. ***Surrealism is litterature*** [sic] w***ith wrong means, not painting, therefore wrong.*** <u>Merzbild Alf.</u> Schwitters *had always insisted that the individual potency of his materials should be effaced in the process of picture-making,* but in 1937-39 *his very untypical interest in* objets trouvés and *the blatant literal presence of objects themselves* in collages, *grotesque faces and still-life objects* in certain paintings *in the new* Pointilliste *style,* late reliefs including *smooth biomorphic forms,* and a *general shift to illusionistic space and organic, curvilinear elements* are ascribed variously to the influence of *1930s Surrealism* or to *the influence of natural scenery* after his move to Norway. What critics who point with seeming surprise at such *inconsistencies* don't seem to realize is that Schwitters was only concerned with consistency *within* each work. DO I CONTRADICT MYSELF? VERY WELL THEN I CONTRADICT MYSELF, (I AM LARGE, I CONTAIN MULTITUDES.) DEINE DESANCTIFICATION IST TÄGLICHEN AUFGEBAUT WIE KASPAR WORDSWORTH ODER FRIEDRICH MACIUNAS, SCHACKO BLUEMNER ODER ANNA BLUME. Schwitters's mind and practice roved freely over all the possibilities available to artists during the first half of the 20th century. ***Combine all branches of art into an artistic unity. <u>Mz 33. Verbürgt rein.</u>*** **We see in his work not only the picture of a new** instinctive order but a picture of its creation: since the material components that create this order are drawn from quite an opposite state, the tension and competitions between parts and whole are necessarily given along with the new order itself. His works transcended his conscious abstract-art ideology, embodying a much more complete theory of art, though he might have been chagrined if told *they imitate nature in its complexity.* THE LARGER LATE ASSEMBLAGES AND COLLAGES, ESPECIALLY, HAVE A FORTHRIGHTNESS AND GENEROSITY ABOUT THEM THAT MAKES THE PRECEDING, CONSTRUCTIVIST-STYLE WORK SEEM OVERCONTROLLED BY CONTRAST. *Der Schokaladenkasten, Anna Blume, Box 7.* He feared *inexactness lest it fall into mere* RANDOMNESS. **Even close friends found it difficult to reconcile Schwitters' jovial, extrovert, and clownish nature with the seriousness of his commitment to art.** The liveliness of Schwitters' art may well have arisen from the widely noted *contradictoriness of his existence,* and that very *contradictoriness* prevented MERZ from becoming an ideology, allowing him to embrace a myriad of materials and methods and to approach, willy-nilly, *imitating nature in its manner of operation.* **DO NOT ASK FOR SOULFUL MOODS.** THE DADAIST IS A MIRROR CARRIER. *There is no such thing as inchoate experience.* Perception is always already preconstituted by the perceiver. **A Merzer met Roof on the roof.** One may respect, like, enjoy, or be delighted or even made ecstatic by the works of a number of artists, but those of a few--in this centuury Stein, Satie, and Schwitters, Klee and Cage, and still inescapably Schoenberg, and not a large handful of pothers--one loves. *Industriegebiet. Aq. 37.* **The Cathedral broke through the ceiling and aspiring upward pushed into Kurt's and Helma's apartment above, leaving one of the rooms with no floor.** *Merzbau Hannover,* begun by Schwitters around 1923 and continually worked upon for nearly fourteen years, was twenty years later--five years before his death--destroyed by Allied bombs. *During the 1930s Schwitters often worked day and night on his useless construction.* Merzbau in Little Langdale (Merz Barn). On New Year's Day 1937 (ten months before this Merzer began writing poems) Schwitters left Germany, never again *to* see *Merzbau Hannover,* and that year began the second *Merzbau,* in Lysaker, Norway, which was destroyed by fire in 1951; ten years after beginning the second and six months before he died, he began the third and last *Merzbau* (the *Merz Barn*) on Cylinder's Farm in Little Langdale, near Ambleside, in the Lake District of England, the one more or less completed wall of which, though moved, still survives. Oh, **Du,** Kurt Schwitters, **Du!**

[With special thanks to Nick Piombino (poet, poeticist, psychoanalyst), who kindly lent the poet his Schwitters library, notably the two books most often quoted, adapted, excerpted, paraphrased, etc., in the course of constructing this *Merzgedicht*: Werner Schmalenbach's *Kurt Schwitters* (Copyright 1967 in West Germany by Verlag M. DuMont Schauberg, Cologne; English version published by Harry N. Abrams, Inc., New York, 1977) and John Elderfield's *Kurt Schwitters* (Copyright (c) 1985 by Thames and Hudson Ltd., London; paperback edition specially printed for the Museum of Modern Art, New York, by Thames and Hudson Inc., New York, 1985), to the authors and publishers of which the poet is grateful for the many scattered sentences and shorter excerpts informally quoted, paraphrased, adapted, and/or modified throughout this poem; and with special thanks to Michael Erlhoff and Klaus Stadtmüller, the editors of the *Kurt Schwitters Almanach 1987* (a birth-centennial "Hommage à Kurt Schwitters") for inviting me to send them a contribution, inspiring me to write this poem.   JML]

February - March 1987
New York

2nd Merzgedicht in Memoriam Kurt Schwitters

love and hate everything

Striving for expression in a work of art seems to   *me injurious*
to art.

    infinity   *that is correct*

MerzMerzbild

letters

artworks

Schwitters

Art as simple as writing the
letter i.

excitement brought on St. Vitus's dance

love and hate everything

Dada was ideological without a   *specific*
ideology and purposive without a purpose,   *which is why Dada actions*
and objects could be   *considered* artistic.

Schwitters shied away

illusionistic

Tzara

indifferently

conventional

A marvelous dilettante

Schwitters

                                        Chanson des autres
                                is i.

Merz
            letters

  Realism made from real things

Chicago
                            him nonpolitical because he
            espoused no easily recognized ideology

                                unaltered found materials
            possibly

CONTEMPLATIVE

                                        whatever has been taken
                                for granted
            Merz

                        artworks

  backward
                                        artworks
                    printing
    Entformung

  There is no such thing as inchoate experience.

                        praxis

            The Cathedral broke through the
ceiling and aspiring upward pushed into Kurt's and
                Helma's apartment above,
            leaving one of the rooms
                        with no floor.

        Urbegriff

                                blatant literal
                                                    GESTURES
                    presence
                                    of
        objects   Huelsenbeck

        ONE CAN EVEN SHOUT OUT THROUGH REFUSE

                            7

Aphorismer

Schwitters

Hannover strives
forward

world everything

aufgebaut

Aphorismer

Komposition

nonpolitical because

he espoused no easily recognized

ideology

occasionally

DO OTHERWISE

SCHWITTERS SHIED AWAY

paradise

Merz ist form

familiar reality

that is correct

infinity

man-made hill

GESTURES

ecstatic

SCHWITTERS SHIED AWAY

Malerei

Go out into the whole world and make the truth known,
the only truth there is,　　　　　　*the truth*
　　　　　　　　　　　　　　　　　　about Anna Blume.

Realism made
from　　　**I love and hate**
everything　　　　　　　　　　　　　　*real*
things

that is correct

artworks

contradictoriness

delighted

illusionistic space

Realism made
from real   *avant-garde*

things

smooth biomorphic forms

nothing outside itself

bicycle   *Entformung,*

Eigengift, konsequent, Urbegriff.

Eigengift

The materials bring   *into the*
abstract formal performance a piece of   *familiar reality.*

discarded unfinished pages

<u>*something or other*</u> ***Frühe***

printed matter

A consistent work of Art   **as**

simple as writing the letter i.

art

he didn't care

Why

make artworks if you're

opposed to art?

A r t   i s   a u t o n o m o u s.

ties

regarded words

consistent work of

because   A

bautze

needless

art

die Brocken des täglichen Abfalls

desanctification
head

AN IMAGE OF THE REVOLUTION

he couldn't sleep

articulated

A r t   i s   a u t o n o m o u s.

Schwitters

dying   *delicately*

use anything

conventional

DO NOT ASK FOR SOULFUL MOODS.

avant-garde

each discarded bit or

Sᴄʜᴡɪᴛᴛᴇʀs sʜɪᴇᴅ ᴀᴡᴀʏ

snippet

because

Hannover   Space

There is no such thing as inchoate *experience.*

Chicago *Malerei*

*Kom*MERZ *und Privatbank.*

SCHWITTERS SHIED AWAY

Merzideology

symbols

illusionis

tic space

wooden

an artist's loft

except those on the top of GESTURES

The Cathedral broke through the ceiling and **aspiring upward**
pushed into Kurt's and **Helma's**
apartment above, **leaving one of** **the rooms with no floor.**

DADAISTS

Chanson des autres is i.

+ *ONE CAN EVEN SHOUT OUT*
THROUGH REFUSE, AND THIS IS WHAT I DID, NAILING AND GLUING

ALWAYS

nonpolitical because he espoused no easily
recognized ideology

man-made hill

logic and grammar

SELF-ABSORPTION

blatant literal presence of objects
Id

Schwitters Schwitters

11

Hannover

discarded unfinished pages

artworks

Schwitters

ideology

agency

destroyed by Allied

bombs

in Hannover

familiar reality

parrot

lights   **bautze**

praxis   *illusionistic*

illusionistic

ecstatic   paradise

all night   an artist's loft
                                    death

infinity

Du!

Combine all branches of art into an artistic

FLUXUS   **unity.**

Merz   FRAGMENTS

antiartistic

THE MOST INTERNATIONAL PETIT BOURGEOIS IN THE WORLD.

mere RANDOMNESS

Komposition

an artist's loft

complexity

distancing

FORTHRIGHTNESS AND GENEROSITY

A r t i s a u t o n o m o u s.

Chanson des autres is i.

death

an art attitude

praxis

The Cathedral broke through the ceiling and aspiring upward pushed into Kurt's and Helma's apartment above, leaving one of the rooms with no floor.

political

the new order   *FRAGMENTS*

destroyed by Allied bombs

trouble

experience allows her to see

a pure image maker

Art as simple as writing the letter i.   them

Elikan merzed a konsequent brocken.

Chanson des autres is i.

letters

A r t i s a u t o n o m o u s.

13

smooth biomorphic forms

Hannover

contradictoriness   *strives*
                                                                                                        forward

Schwitters

he couldn't sleep

THE MOST INTERNATIONAL PETIT

BOURGEOIS IN THE WORLD.

stupidity of institutions

illusionistic space

Realism made from real things

ELIKAN MERZED A KONSEQUENT BROCKEN.

A consistent work of art

supposedly antiartistic

delighted

I love and hate everything

**The Cathedral broke through the ceiling   and
aspiring upward pushed into Kurt's and Helma's   apartment above, leaving one of
the rooms with no
floor.**

the end of all
chagrined

Entformun,

Eigengift, konsequent, Urbegriff.

Realism made from real things

very large collages

use anything

Why make artworks if you're
opposed to art?

whatever has been taken for granted

blatant literal **logic**

and grammar *presence of*
objects

complexity unaltered found materials

FORTHRIGHTNESS AND GENEROSITY

paradise

experience allows her to see them

Go out into the whole world and make the truth known, *the only*
truth there is, the truth about Anna Blume.

23 - 28 March 1987
New York

15

3rd Merzgedicht in Memoriam Kurt Schwitters

paradise

A consistent work of art

pain

desanctification

illusionistic

experience allows her to see them

Realism made from real things

18 April 1987
New York

4th Merzgedicht in Memoriam *Kurt Schwitters*

sees itself reaching the end of all intensifications

Never believed he was making anything but pure abstract forms

as tolerant as possible with respect to its material

TYLL EULENSPIEGEL

DO NOT ASK FOR SOULFUL MOODS.

TYLL EULENSPIEGEL

DO NOT ASK FOR SOULFUL MOODS.

increasing formalization

18 April 1987
New York

5th Merzgedicht in Memoriam Kurt Schwitters

Hannover

REFUSE

TÄGLICHEN AUFGEBAUT WIE KASPAR WORDSWORTH ODER FRIEDRICH MACIUNAS, SCHACKO BLUEMNER ODER ANNA BLUME. Schwitters's mind and practice roved freely over all the possibilities available to artists.

Cage

Schoenberg

desanctification

use anything to make art
A MARVELOUS DILETTANTE

18 April 1987
New York

6th Merzgedicht in Memoriam *Kurt Schwitters*

the end of all

Dadaists

only concerned with consistency *within* each work.

A consistent work of art

fantastic

MADNESS OR A BAD JOKE TURNS INTO A SOLID CULTURAL   POSSESSION

fantastic

political

only concerned with consistency *within* each work.
Merz ist form.

Realism made from real things

objets trouvés

political

FRAGMENTS

Schwitters and Wordsworth lived their last years, died, and are buried--4 miles from each other--in England's Lake District.

experience

dying

he couldn't sleep

TÄGLICHEN AUFGEBAUT WIE KASPAR WORDSWORTH ODER FRIEDRICH MACIUNAS, SCHACKO BLUEMNER ODER ANNA BLUME. Schwitters's mind and practice roved freely over all the possibilities available to artists.

ART NEEDS CONTEMPLATIVE SELF-ABSORPTION.

beginning

artworks

AN IMAGE OF THE REVOLUTION

Komposition
seriousness

*Kom*MERZ *und Privatbank.*

continually worked upon for nearly fourteen years

Maciunas

sees itself reaching the end of all
intensifications

paradise

Chanson des autres is i.

18 April 1987
New York

7th Merzgedicht in Memoriam *Kurt Schwitters*

wooden

excitement brought on St.
Vitus's dance

Satie

logic and grammar

indifferently

MY BASIC TRAIT IS

MELANCHOLY.

an artist's loft

discarded unfinished pages

told *they imitate nature in its complexity.*

antiartistic

aufgebaut

THE DADAIST IS   A
MIRROR CARRIER.

Rumpelstiltskin

Merzbild

18 April 1987
New York

8th Merzgedicht in Memoriam Kurt Schwitters

smooth biomorphic forms
avant-garde   each discarded bit or snippet
praxis   the most banal detritus
Never believed he was making anything but pure abstract
forms.   unaltered found materials
Komposition   pain
ideology   respect, like, enjoy, or be
delighted   *Entformung, Eigengift,*
konsequent, Urbegriff.
Schwitters maintained
that a reproduction could be as good as an original and
painted a number of pictures in more than one copy.
delighted   <u>reclining emm.</u>   he couldn't sleep
Schwitters maintained that a reproduction could be
as good as an original and painted a number of
pictures in more than one copy.
regarded words and letters both as meaningful
symbols and as formal design elements
REFUSE   *Malerei*
The materials bring into the abstract formal   performance a piece of familiar
reality.
SOULFUL   Schwitters's mind and practice
roved freely.   **A MARVELOUS DILETTANTE**
Schwitters reveals himself as a naive utopian.
Now I call myself **Merz.**
SCHWITTERS WENT SO FAR AS TO DISCARD THE IDEA THAT
A   PICTURE IS A UNIQUE CREATION.   *bring*
into the abstract formal performance a
piece of familiar reality. objets trouvés
Schwitters's mind and practice roved freely.
peace   Merz   *In the early days of*
Merz his position was anti-functionalist, purely
artistic: a utopian conception.

blatant literal presence of objects
Schwitters maintained that a reproduction could be
as good as an original and painted a number of
pictures **in more than one copy.**
Art needs contemplative self-absorption.
SCHWITTERS DISMISSED THE IMPORTANCE ATTACHED TO A
PICTURE'S INDIVIDUAL CHARACTERISTICS AS
sentimentalism. *Komposition*
Rumpelstiltskin
reclining emm. *familiar reality political*
respect, like, enjoy, or be delighted
My *basic trait is melancholy.*
peace Schoenberg
Rumpelstiltskin **seriousness**
something or other. Frühe whatever has been
taken for granted may begin to be questioned and
eventually illumined
told *they imitate nature in its complexity.*
Construction for Noble Ladies.
In the early days of Merz his position was
anti-functionalist, purely *artistic: a utopian*
conception. Ambleside
violet *indifferently Merzbild*
lawfully allowed time **a picture of its**
creation *blatant literal presence of objects*
Merz ist form. Never believed he was making anything but pure
abstract forms.
Never believed he was making anything but pure
abstract forms. each discarded bit or
snippet *entirely without*
bourgeois comforts
Space

continually worked upon for nearly fourteen years
supposedly antiartistic *Schwitters'*
expressive power was given direction by the scraps
with which he created forms. **Chanson des**
autres is i. *political*
Never believed he was making anything but pure
abstract forms.
Schwitters reveals
himself as a naive utopian.
I love and hate everything. *ALWAYS DO OTHERWISE THAN*
THE OTHERS.

ecstatic   conventional   *contradictoriness*

> ***My wet nurse's milk was too thick and there***
> ***was too little, because she nursed me beyond***
> ***the lawfully allowed time.***

Lysaker   **It was not only because they**
could   serve as well as painter's pigment that
Schwitters   **made use of the**
residues of life, the   **wretchedest of all**
materials.   *that is*   *correct* **It**
was not only because they could serve as   well as
painter's pigment that Schwitters made use of
      the residues of life, the wretchedest of all
materials.   *familiar reality*

          Satie   **SOULFUL**

      something or other. **Frühe**

          a picture of its creation
totally disabled   he couldn't sleep

by his very nature he was Dada   *excitement*
                    brought on St. Vitus's dance   *by*
his very nature he was Dada   Lysaker
   against war

          Schwitters shied away.

everything   love and hate

Chanson des autres is i.
the tension and competitions between parts and whole
   Blau ist die Farbe Deines gelben Haares.
Hannover   *Hannover strives forward*   unaltered
found materials   *My wet nurse's milk was too thick*
and there   *was too little, because she nursed*
me beyond   *the lawfully allowed time.*
   excitement
respect, like, enjoy, or be delighted

   Lysaker   dying   ***THE DADAIST***
IS   ***A MIRROR CARRIER.***   *Striving for*
expression in a work of art seems to me injurious
   to art.   *stupidity of institutions*

   pain

objets trouvés   *The most international*
petit bourgeois in the world.   ***REFUSE***
complexity   **unaltered found materials**
   Schwitters' jovial, extrovert, and clownish
   nature   carefully cropped details from   printers' reject
material
   Merzbau Hannover, begun by Schwitters around 1923 and
   continually workcd upon for nearly fourteen years,
   was twenty years later--five years before
his death--destroyed by Allied bombs. whatever has been
taken for granted may begin to be questioned and
eventually   illumined   *Striving for*
expression in a work of   *art seems to me*
injurious to art.   *excitement brought on*
St. Vitus's dance
   the end of all
   probably in New York gather them into the
   paradise of art's *Urbegriff*
   excitement *familiar reality*   Id   Space
   Hannover strives forward
discarded unfinished pages   praxis

logic and grammar supposedly antiartistic
gather them into the paradise of art's *Urbegriff*

familiar reality   *as tolerant as*
possible with respect to its material
the   **new order**   objets trouvés
                hovers between the extremes of regularity
and   predictability on the one hand and
disorder on the   other
Schwitters' expressive   *power was given*
direction by the scraps with which he
created forms.   *In the early days*
                of Merz his position was anti-functionalist,
purely *artistic: a utopian conception.*
     Tyll Eulenspiegel   Dadaism as an
                advertising   delighted   *Verbürgt rein.*

NATURE, FROM THE LATIN NASCI, I.E., TO BECOME OR
COME INTO BEING, EVERYTHING THAT THROUGH ITS OWN FORCE
DEVELOPS, FORMS OR MOVES.   antiartistic
Hannover strives forward   imitating nature in its
     manner of operation   sleep
<u>**Art needs contemplative self-absorption.**</u>

     sleep   *Malerei*   scorned or scoffed
at   **loosening its ties to art**
<u>**Art needs contemplative self-absorption.**</u>
          Schwitters' expressive power was given direction
by   *the scraps with which he created forms.*
          Verbürgt rein.   **love**
               and hate everything   *Striving for*
expression in a work of art seems to me injurious to art.

whatever has been taken for granted may begin to be
questioned and eventually illumined
delighted   chagrined
Maciunas   only concerned with consistency *within*
each   work.   Id   *There*
is no such thing as inchoate experience.
reclining emm.
carefully cropped details from printers'
reject material
Lysaker
A MARVELOUS DILETTANTE   *illusionistic*
space   Dada was ideological without a specific
ideology and purposive without a purpose, which is
why Dada actions and objects could be considered
artistic.   Dadaists   **Schwitters'**
jovial, extrovert, and clownish nature
that is correct   **MIRROR**
SOULFUL

conventional

artworks   *THE DADAIST IS A MIRROR CARRIER.*
dying   each discarded bit or snippet
mere randomness   *THE DADAIST IS A*
MIRROR CARRIER.   *by his very nature he was*
Dada   a pure image maker
NATURE, FROM THE LATIN NASCI, I.E., TO BECOME OR COME
INTO BEING, EVERYTHING THAT THROUGH ITS OWN FORCE
DEVELOPS, FORMS OR MOVES.   *entirely without*

bourgeois comforts
A   t   s   u   o   o   o   s   .
r   i   a   t   n   m   u   .
SOULFUL
Satie   **Schwitters' jovial,**
extrovert, and clownish nature
against war   **One can even shout out**
through refuse.

Satie   Schwitters reveals
himself as a naive utopian.   *Entformung,*
Eigengift, konsequent, Urbegriff.
trouble   he couldn't sleep

Art needs contemplative self-absorption.

Now it is a Merzpicture. Sorry!   Space

DO NOT ASK FOR SOULFUL MOODS.   *AN IMAGE OF*

THE REVOLUTION   each discarded bit or

snippet   *Merzbau Hannover*

him nonpolitical because he espoused no easily

recognized ideology   Satie   *smooth*

biomorphic forms   unaltered found

materials   experience

allows her to see them   This was before H.R.H.

The Late Duke   of

Clarence &

Avondale. Now it is a Merzpicture. Sorry!

sleep   preconstituted

discarded unfinished pages

avant-garde   Schwitters reveals himself as

a naive utopian.   *fantastic*

dying   Stein

Lake   reclining emm.

the most banal detritus   the most banal

detritus   embodying a much more complete

theory

My basic trait is melancholy.   him

nonpolitical because he espoused no easily recognized

ideology   only concerned with

consistency *within* each work.   *inchoate*

experience   *infinity*   letters

lawfully allowed time   *Combine all*

branches of art into an artistic unity. *complexity*

as tolerant as possible with respect to its

material

FORTHRIGHTNESS AND GENEROSITY   Tzara

in a strange context   *THE MOST*

INTERNATIONAL petit bourgeois *IN THE WORLD.*   gather

them into the   paradise of art's

Urbegriff   whatever   has been taken

for granted may begin to be   questioned

and eventually illumined

inchoate experience   supposedly antiartistic
experience allows her to see them   *There*
is   *no such thing as inchoate experience.*   *meine süsse*
puppe,
mir ist alles schnuppe,
wenn ich meine schnauze
auf die deine bautze.

24 - 29 June 1987
New York

9th Merzgedicht in Memoriam *Kurt Schwitters*

an art attitude
Rot ist die Farbe Deines grünen Vogels.

each discarded bit or snippet
Never believed he was making anything but pure abstract forms.

A   t   s   u   o   o   s.
 r   i   a   t   n   m   u

regarded words and letters both as meaningful symbols and as formal design elements
familiar reality
paradise
wooden
art seems to me injurious to art
totally disabled
familiar reality
commitment to art
<u>reclining emm.</u>

regarded words and letters both as meaningful symbols and as formal design elements
Hannover
antiartistic
continually worked upon for nearly fourteen years
writing poems
Schwitters
Combine all branches of art into an artistic unity.

Schwitters
Merzbau Hannover Dadaism as an advertising
loosening its ties to art
Schwitters' expressive power was given direction by the scraps with which he created forms.

writing poems
love and hate everything
letters
that is correct
loosening its ties to art
trouble
paradise
UNALTERED FOUND MATERIALS
destroyed by Allied bombs
Verbürgt rein.

fragments
delighted
DO NOT ASK FOR SOULFUL MOODS.

Tzara
Merzbau Hannover, begun by Schwitters around 1923 and continually worked upon for
nearly fourteen years, was twenty years later--five years before his death--destroyed by
Allied bombs.

transcended his conscious abstract-art ideology
Rot ist die Farbe Deines grünen Vogels.

Merzbau Hannover
transcended his conscious abstract-art ideology
Schwitters
Combine all branches of art into an artistic unity.

preconstituted
avant-garde
ecstatic
antiartistic
use anything
I love and hate everything.

pain
completed wall
blatant literal presence of objects
stupidity of institutions
Striving for expression in a work of art seems to me injurious to art.

Schwitters' method is that of Realism made from real things.

familiar reality
illusionistic space
very large collages
This was before H.R.H. The Late Duke of Clarence & Avondale.

Now it is a Merzpicture.   Sorry!

A typical Schwitters collage, such as Mz 271 Kammer [Cupboard], combines the formal stability of the grid format with carefully plotted diagonal movements that enliven the rectilinear geometry without diminishing its solidity.

Merzbild
whatever has been taken for granted
totally disabled
artworks
Merzbild **seriousness**
Id
paradise
by his very nature he was Dada
AVOID: BECOMING THE CLASSICS OF TOMORROW
Hannover
AN IMAGE OF THE REVOLUTION
experience
It was not only because they could serve as well as painter's pigment that Schwitters
made use of the residues of life, the wretchedest of all materials.

AN IMAGE OF THE REVOLUTION
logic and grammar
something or other. *Frühe*
A consistent work of art
commitment to art
trouble
a pure image maker
Chicago
Never believed he was making anything but pure abstract forms.

Satie
entirely without bourgeois comforts
ideology
Tyll Eulenspiegel
Combine all branches of art into an artistic unity.

infinity
continually worked upon for nearly fourteen years
infinity
love and hate everything love and hate everything
preconstituted
Tyll Eulenspiegel
Combine all branches of art into an artistic unity.

love and hate everything
avant-garde
ecstatic
infinity
preconstituted
Du!

love and hate everything
preconstituted
avant-garde
fantastic
death
letters
use anything.

A r t   i s   a u t o n o m o u s .

love and hate everything
letters sleep
Komposition
stupidity of institutions
letters
Entformung, Eigengift, konsequent, Urbegriff.

use anything
death
love and hate everything
täglichen aufgebaut wie Kaspar Wordsworth oder Friedrich Maciunas, Schacko
Bluemner oder Anna Blume. Schwitters' mind and practice roved freely over all the
possibilities available to artists.

stupidity of institutions
familiar reality
illusionistic
illusionistic space
Entformung, Eigengift, konsequent, Urbegriff.

bring into the abstract formal performance a piece of familiar reality.

close friends found it difficult to reconcile Schwitters
THE MOST INTERNATIONAL petit bourgeois *IN THE WORLD.*

love and hate everything
THE MOST INTERNATIONAL petit bourgeois *IN THE WORLD.*

meine süsse puppe,
mir ist alles schnuppe,
wenn ich meine schnauze
auf die deine bautze.

illusionistic space
Lake
Merzbild
THE MOST INTERNATIONAL petit bourgeois *IN THE WORLD.*

Now I call myself **Merz.**

illusionistic space
discarded unfinished pages
illusionistic
illusionistic space **Art as simple as writing the letter** *i.*

love and hate everything
whatever has been taken for granted
Schwitters's mind and practice roved freely
him nonpolitical because he espoused no easily recognized ideology
indifferently
Id
discarded unfinished pages
FORTHRIGHTNESS AND GENEROSITY
Chanson des autres is **i.**

Rumpelstiltskin
Hannover strives forward
DO NOT ASK FOR SOULFUL MOODS.

him nonpolitical because he espoused no easily recognized ideology
totally disabled
artistic unity
DO NOT ASK FOR SOULFUL MOODS.

preconstituted
Merz
whatever has been taken for granted
Merzbild
love and hate everything
FORTHRIGHTNESS AND GENEROSITY
Schwitters and Wordsworth lived their last years, died, and are buried--4 miles from each other--in England's Lake District.

FORTHRIGHTNESS AND GENEROSITY
beginning
AN IMAGE OF THE REVOLUTION
experience
FORTHRIGHTNESS AND GENEROSITY
My wet nurse's milk was too thick and there was too little, because she nursed me beyond the lawfully allowed time.

Schwitters' expressive power was given direction by the scraps with which he created forms.

by his very nature he was Dada
In the early days of Merz his position was anti-functionalist, purely artistic: a utopian conception.

love and hate everything
experience
In the early days of Merz his position was anti-functionalist, purely artistic: a utopian conception.

REFUSE
the end of all
trouble
A consistent work of art
experience
a pure image maker
People such as Huelsenbeck
scorned or scoffed at
logic and grammar
experience
the end of all
trouble
AN IMAGE OF THE REVOLUTION **love and hate everything**
a pure image maker
Schoenberg
pain
an art attitude
Chicago
Satie
Schoenberg
dying
pain
Satie
Schoenberg
commitment to art
antiartistic
The Cathedral broke through the ceiling and aspiring upward pushed into Kurt's and Helma's apartment above, leaving one of the rooms with no floor.

Schwitters
Cage
antiartistic
fantastic
avant-garde
avant-garde
regarded words and letters both as meaningful symbols and as formal design elements
Tyll Eulenspiegel
mere randomness
ecstatic
fantastic
sleep death
Schwitters
Combine all branches of art into an artistic unity.

letters
completed wall
The Cathedral broke through the ceiling and aspiring upward pushed into Kurt's and Helma's apartment above, leaving one of the rooms with no floor.

A r t i s   a u t o n o m o u s .

death
The Cathedral broke through the ceiling and aspiring upward pushed into Kurt's and Helma's apartment above, leaving one of the rooms with no floor.

Combine all branches of art into an artistic unity.

Schwitters
ecstatic
fantastic
conventional
experience allows her to see them
täglichen aufgebaut wie Kaspar Wordsworth oder Friedrich Maciunas, Schacko Bluemner oder Anna Blume. Schwitters' mind and practice roved freely over all the possibilities available to artists.

Komposition
Hannover strives forward
blatant literal presence of objects
sleep
death
conventional
experience allows her to see them
Hannover strives forward
him nonpolitical because he espoused no easily recognized ideology
Huelsenbeck
man-made hill
experience allows her to see them
man-made hill
wooden
Schwitters maintained that a reproduction could be as good as an original and painted a number of pictures in more than one copy.

There is no such thing as inchoate experience.

Huelsenbeck
man-made hill
Hannover strives forward
conventional
seriousness
The Cathedral broke through the ceiling and aspiring upward pushed into Kurt's and Helma's apartment above, leaving one of the rooms with no floor.

Schwitters
fantastic
conventional
experience allows her to see them
only concerned with consistency *within* each work.

Dadaists
death
Du!

conventional
täglichen aufgebaut wie Kaspar Wordsworth oder Friedrich Maciunas, Schacko Bluemner oder Anna Blume. Schwitters' mind and practice roved freely over all the possibilities available to artists.

Schwitters' method is that of Realism made from real things.

THE DADAIST IS A MIRROR CARRIER.

only concerned with consistency *within* each work.

Schwitters
Hannover strives forward
THE DADAIST IS A MIRROR CARRIER.

in a strange context
THE DADAIST IS A MIRROR CARRIER.

Hannover strives forward
in a strange context
in a strange context
THE DADAIST IS A MIRROR CARRIER.

Schwitters
illusionistic
chagrined
destroyed by Allied bombs
objets trouvés
chagrined
destroyed by Allied bombs
desanctification
meine süsse puppe,
mir ist alles schnuppe,
wenn ich meine schnauze
auf die deine bautze.

gather them into the paradise of art's *Urbegriff*
objets trouvés
experience allows her to see them
Schwitters
only concerned with consistency *within* each work.

chagrined
illusionistic
a picture of its creation
each discarded bit or snippet
blatant literal presence of objects
antiartistic
difficult to reconcile
conventional
illusionistic
in a strange context
täglichen aufgebaut wie Kaspar Wordsworth oder Friedrich Maciunas, Schacko Bluemner oder Anna Blume. Schwitters' mind and practice roved freely over all the possibilities available to artists.

objets trouvés
a picture of its creation
illusionistic
experience allows her to see them
Schwitters
Merz
UNALTERED FOUND MATERIALS
Realism made from real things
A typical Schwitters collage, such as Mz 271 Kammer [Cupboard]*, combines the formal stability of the grid format with carefully plotted diagonal movements that enliven the rectilinear geometry without diminishing its solidity.*

DO NOT ASK FOR SOULFUL MOODS.

DO NOT ASK FOR SOULFUL MOODS.

Merz
THE DADAIST IS A MIRROR CARRIER.

Realism made from real things
UNALTERED FOUND MATERIALS
Merz
Hannover strives forward
in a strange context
DO NOT ASK FOR SOULFUL MOODS.

Schwitters
him nonpolitical because he espoused no easily recognized ideology
One can even shout out through refuse.

bring into the abstract formal performance a piece of familiar reality.

Verbürgt rein.

him nonpolitical because he espoused no easily recognized ideology
indifferently
aufgebaut
Schwitters and Wordsworth lived their last years, died, and are buried--4 miles from each
other--in England's Lake District.

There is no such thing as inchoate experience.

One can even shout out through refuse.

meine süsse puppe,
mir ist alles schnuppe,
wenn ich meine schnauze
auf die deine bautze.

Schwitters' jovial, extrovert, and clownish nature
Schwitters dismissed the importance attached to a picture's individual characteristics as
sentimentalism.

seriousness
familiar reality
blatant literal presence of objects
Schwitters
Schwitters
praxis
fragments
Elikan merzed a konsequent brocken.

Fluxus
in a strange context
Realism made from real things
UNALTERED FOUND MATERIALS
DO NOT ASK FOR SOULFUL MOODS.

praxis
fragments
Elikan merzed a konsequent brocken.

delighted
The materials bring into the abstract formal performance a piece of familiar reality.

ecstatic
A typical Schwitters collage, such as <u>Mz 271 Kammer</u> [Cupboard]*, combines the formal stability of the grid format with carefully plotted diagonal movements that enliven the rectilinear geometry without diminishing its solidity.*

Schwitters
REFUSE
A MARVELOUS DILETTANTE
REFUSE
the end of all
Dada was ideological without a specific ideology and purposive without a purpose, which is why Dada actions and objects could be considered artistic.

A MARVELOUS DILETTANTE
ALWAYS DO OTHERWISE THAN THE OTHERS.

respect, like, enjoy, or be delighted
*Kom*MERZ *und Privatbank.*
in a strange context
Hannover strives forward
<u>violet</u>
political
the end of all
REFUSE
There is no such thing as inchoate experience.

antiartistic
difficult to reconcile
<u>reclining emm.</u>

probably in New York
I love and hate everything.

use anything
letters
very large collages
each discarded bit or snippet
Ambleside
Art needs contemplative self-absorption.

complexity
each discarded bit or snippet
a picture of its creation
Ambleside
each discarded bit or snippet
Art needs contemplative self-absorption.

antiartistic
use anything
very large collages
I love and hate everything.

illusionistic
objets trouvés
fantastic
avant-garde
sleep
death
pain
an art attitude
death
Ambleside
infinity
THE MOST INTERNATIONAL petit bourgeois *IN THE WORLD.*

antiartistic
avant-garde
desanctification
a picture of its creation
completed wall
sleep
The Cathedral broke through the ceiling and aspiring upward pushed into Kurt's and Helma's apartment above, leaving one of the rooms with no floor.

Ambleside
desanctification
meine süsse puppe,
mir ist alles schnuppe,
wenn ich meine schnauze
auf die deine bautze.

MIRROR
excitement
transcended his conscious abstract-art ideology
Rot ist die Farbe Deines grünen Vogels.

Lysaker
NATURE, FROM THE LATIN NASCI, I.E., TO BECOME OR COME INTO BEING, EVERYTHING THAT THROUGH ITS OWN FORCE DEVELOPS, FORMS OR MOVES.

praxis
fragments
imitating nature in its manner of operation
One can even shout out through refuse, and this is what I did, nailing and gluing.

desanctification
meine süsse puppe,
mir ist alles schnuppe,
wenn ich meine schnauze
auf die deine bautze.

Hannover
against war
beginning In the early days of Merz his position was anti-functionalist, purely artistic: a utopian conception.

sleep
fragments
avant-garde
excitement
MIRROR
familiar reality
Schwitters
antiartistic
avant-garde
death
sleep
a picture of its creation
each discarded bit or snippet
The Cathedral broke through the ceiling and aspiring upward pushed into Kurt's and Helma's apartment above, leaving one of the rooms with no floor.

avant-garde
The Cathedral broke through the ceiling and aspiring upward pushed into Kurt's and Helma's apartment above, leaving one of the rooms with no floor.

Ambleside
Art needs contemplative self-absorption.

only concerned with consistency *within* each work.

bring into the abstract formal performance a piece of familiar reality.

51

gather them into the paradise of art's *Urbegriff*
completed wall
Ambleside
Art needs contemplative self-absorption.

familiar reality
antiartistic
blatant literal presence of objects
only concerned with consistency *within* each work.

Dadaists
bring into the abstract formal performance a piece of familiar reality.

each discarded bit or snippet
destroyed by Allied bombs
chagrined
antiartistic
Dadaists
only concerned with consistency *within* each work.

complexity
This was before H.R.H. The Late Duke of Clarence & Avondale.

Now it is a Merzpicture.   Sorry!

bring into the abstract formal performance a piece of familiar reality.

gather them into the paradise of art's *Urbegriff*
Dadaists
Art needs contemplative self-absorption.

antiartistic
each discarded bit or snippet
This was before H.R.H. The Late Duke of Clarence & Avondale.

Now it is a Merzpicture.   Sorry!

he couldn't sleep
whatever has been taken for granted may begin to be questioned and eventually illumined
art seems to me injurious to art
Now I call myself **Merz**.

Now I call myself **Merz**.

art seems to me injurious to art
he couldn't sleep
antiartistic
A typical Schwitters collage, such as Mz 271 Kammer [Cupboard]*, combines the formal stability of the grid format with carefully plotted diagonal movements that enliven the rectilinear geometry without diminishing its solidity.*

familiar reality
antiartistic
familiar reality
A typical Schwitters collage, such as Mz 271 Kammer [Cupboard]*, combines the formal stability of the grid format with carefully plotted diagonal movements that enliven the rectilinear geometry without diminishing its solidity.*

antiartistic
Construction for Noble Ladies.

Schwitters
Schwitters *art seems to me injurious to art*
<u>*Verbürgt rein.*</u>

<u>*Verbürgt rein.*</u>

Schwitters dismissed the importance attached to a picture's individual characteristics as
sentimentalism.

lawfully allowed time
Hannover strives forward
Schwitters maintained that a reproduction could be as good as an original and painted a
number of pictures in more than one copy.

whatever has been taken for granted may begin to be questioned and eventually illumined
he couldn't sleep
Art as simple as writing the letter *i*.

the new order
man-made hill
Huelsenbeck
wooden
Schwitters maintained that a reproduction could be as good as an original and painted a
number of pictures in more than one copy.

seriousness
GESTURES
man-made hill
Schwitters
a picture of its creation
each discarded bit or snippet
<u>**Art needs contemplative self-absorption.**</u>

lawfully allowed time
Hannover strives forward
Schwitters maintained that a reproduction could be as good as an original and painted a number of pictures in more than one copy.

antiartistic
seriousness
familiar reality
Hannover
Hannover antiartistic
antiartistic
seriousness
him nonpolitical because he espoused no easily recognized ideology
each discarded bit or snippet
peace
excitement
MIRROR
man-made hill
Huelsenbeck
Schwitters dismissed the importance attached to a picture's individual characteristics as sentimentalism.

Huelsenbeck
Art needs contemplative self-absorption.

Ambleside
transcended his conscious abstract-art ideology
Rot ist die Farbe Deines grünen Vogels.

NATURE, FROM THE LATIN NASCI, I.E., TO BECOME OR COME INTO BEING, EVERYTHING THAT THROUGH ITS OWN FORCE DEVELOPS, FORMS OR MOVES.

Schwitters' expressive power was given direction by the scraps with which he created forms.

Schwitters maintained that a reproduction could be as good as an original and painted a number of pictures in more than one copy.

wooden
NATURE, FROM THE LATIN NASCI, I.E., TO BECOME OR COME INTO BEING, EVERYTHING THAT THROUGH ITS OWN FORCE DEVELOPS, FORMS OR MOVES.

Lysaker
My wet nurse's milk was too thick and there was too little, because she nursed me beyond the lawfully allowed time.

Schwitters' expressive power was given direction by the scraps with which he created forms.

antiartistic
man-made hill
imitating nature in its manner of operation
NATURE, FROM THE LATIN NASCI, I.E., TO BECOME OR COME INTO BEING, EVERYTHING THAT THROUGH ITS OWN FORCE DEVELOPS, FORMS OR MOVES.

Rot ist die Farbe Deines grünen Vogels.

transcended his conscious abstract-art ideology
Schoenberg
dying
Lysaker
NATURE, FROM THE LATIN NASCI, I.E., TO BECOME OR COME INTO BEING, EVERYTHING THAT THROUGH ITS OWN FORCE DEVELOPS, FORMS OR MOVES.

People such as Huelsenbeck
loosening its ties to art
transcended his conscious abstract-art ideology
Rot ist die Farbe Deines grünen Vogels.

Merzbau Hannover
THE MOST INTERNATIONAL petit bourgeois *IN THE WORLD.*

Rot ist die Farbe Deines grünen Vogels.

antiartistic
Maciunas
contradictoriness
he couldn't sleep
whatever has been taken for granted may begin to be questioned and eventually illumined

Schwitters
<u>Construction for Noble Ladies.</u>

totally disabled
Merzbild
<u>Now it is a Merzpicture.   Sorry!</u>

<u>Now it is a Merzpicture.   Sorry!</u>

as tolerant as possible with respect to its material
whatever has been taken for granted may begin to be questioned and eventually illumined
as tolerant as possible with respect to its material
he couldn't sleep
Go out into the whole world and make the truth known, the only truth there is, the truth about
Anna Blume.

excitement brought on St. Vitus's dance
artistic unity
discarded unfinished pages
Schoenberg
dying
whatever has been taken for granted may begin to be questioned and eventually illumined
he couldn't sleep
<u>Now it is a Merzpicture.   Sorry!</u>

totally disabled
Never believed he was making anything but pure abstract forms.

completed wall
totally disabled
artworks
entirely without bourgeois comforts

The Cathedral broke through the ceiling and aspiring upward pushed into Kurt's and Helma's apartment above, leaving one of the rooms with no floor.

artistic unity
blatant literal presence of objects
the most banal detritus
A typical Schwitters collage, such as Mz 271 Kammer [Cupboard], *combines the formal stability of the grid format with carefully plotted diagonal movements that enliven the rectilinear geometry without diminishing its solidity.*

UNALTERED FOUND MATERIALS
Realism made from real things
Merz
DO NOT ASK FOR SOULFUL MOODS.

Merzbau Hannover, begun by Schwitters around 1923 and continually worked upon for nearly fourteen years, was twenty years later--five years before his death--destroyed by Allied bombs.

My basic trait is melancholy.

Denn in Kanada,
In Amerika
Hoppst die kleine Omama
Immer rinn in den Zinnober,
Immer knüppeldicke rinn,
Hoppst sie unter, hoppst sie ober,
Macht sie stets den dollsten Zinn.

29 - 30 June 1987
New York

10th Merzgedicht in Memoriam *Kurt Schwitters*

MIRROR   *familiar reality*

Art as simple as writing the letter i.   *The*
materials bring into the abstract formal performance a piece of
familiar reality.

excitement brought on St. Vitus's dance
Rumpelstiltskin

that is correct   Merz
   Why make artworks if you're opposed to art?   *The*
materials bring into the abstract formal performance a piece of
familiar reality.

contradictoriness   familiar reality

complexity   <u>Construction for Noble Ladies.</u>

contradictoriness   *familiar reality*

Why make artworks if you're opposed to art?   *The materials bring into the abstract* *formal performance a piece of familiar reality.*

that is correct ~~*Merz*~~

excitement brought on St. Vitus's dance

Rumpelstiltskin

Art as simple as writing the letter i.

The *materials bring into the abstract formal performance a piece of* *familiar reality.*

excitement brought on St. Vitus's dance   Rumpelstiltskin *REFUSE*   <u>Construction for</u>
<u>Noble Ladies.</u>

avant-garde   *Go out into the whole world and make the truth known, the only truth*
there is, the truth about Anna Blume.   Why make artworks if you're opposed to art?
The materials bring into the abstract formal performance a piece of familiar reality.
conventional   *The materials bring into the abstract formal performance a piece of familiar*
reality.

Maciunas embodying a much more complete theory *paradise Merz   experience allows*
her to see them   Go out into the whole world and make the truth known, the only truth
there is, the truth about Anna Blume.

Realism made from real things   **the new order**   *that is correct Merz* him nonpolitical
because he espoused no easily recognized ideology   Rumpelstiltskin

Realism made from real things   **the new order** continually worked upon for nearly
fourteen years   artworks   experience allows her to see them   *Go out into the whole*
world and make the truth known, the only truth there is, the truth about Anna Blume.

Maciunas *artistic unity*   pain **Now I call myself ~~MERZ~~.**   conventional   *The materials bring into the abstract formal performance a piece of familiar reality.*

avant-garde   *Go out into the whole world and make the truth known, the only truth there is, the truth about Anna Blume.* paradise Schwitters and Wordsworth lived their last years, died, and are buried--4 miles from each other--in England's Lake District. *indifferently Merz* conventional Fluxus   *The materials bring into the abstract formal performance a piece of familiar reality.* pain   use anything   **Now I call myself ~~MERZ~~.** **the new order**

 dying Maciunas   **A MARVELOUS DILETTANTE**   *Realism*
 made from real things **EXPERIENCE ALLOWS HER TO SEE THEM**   *Go out into the whole world and make the truth known, the only*
 truth there is, the truth about Anna Blume. **Now I call myself**
 ~~MERZ~~. the new order   UNALTERED FOUND MATERIALS   *Realism*
 made from real things
 Schwitters discarded the idea that ~~a picture is a unique~~
 ~~creation~~.   *PEACE*   the new order   ~~artworks~~
 MIRROR   *The materials bring into the abstract formal*
 performance a piece of familiar reality.   ~~artworks~~ ***Denn in***
 Kanada,
 In Amerika
 Hoppst die kleine Omama
 Immer rinn in den Zinnober,
 Immer knüppeldicke rinn,
 Hoppst sie unter, hoppst sie ober,
 Macht sie stets den dollsten Zinn.   *The materials bring into the abstract formal*
 performance a piece of familiar reality.   *inchoate experience*   *familiar reality*

continually worked upon for nearly fourteen years   A TRADITIONAL
UNDERSTANDING OF ART   *artworks* **avant-garde REFUSE**   *Go out into the whole world and make the truth known, the only truth there is, the truth about Anna Blume.*
Denn in Kanada,
In Amerika
Hoppst die kleine Omama
Immer rinn in den Zinnober,
Immer knüppeldicke rinn,
Hoppst sie unter, hoppst sie ober,
Macht sie stets den dollsten Zinn.   *The materials bring into the abstract formal*
performance a piece of familiar reality.   *inchoate experience*   *familiar reality*

Schwitters discarded the idea that ~~a picture is a unique creation.~~   *PEACE*   **the new order**   artworks Maciunas   trouble ***artistic unity* Now I call myself** ~~**MERZ**~~**.   the new order**   unaltered found materials   *Realism made from real things*

dying Maciunas   **A MARVELOUS DILETTANTE**   *Realism made from real things* *REFUSE*   *contradictoriness* <u>Construction for Noble Ladies.</u> **PARADISE** Schwitters and Wordsworth lived their last years, died, and are buried--4 miles from each other--in England's L ake District.   *indifferently Merz*

PAIN USE ANYTHING   Now I call myself ~~**MERZ**~~**.   the new order   Art as simple as writing the letter** i.   **MIRROR**   *The materials bring into the abstract formal performance a piece of familiar reality.   The materials bring into the abstract formal performance a piece of familiar reality.*   artworks   *Merzbild* Schwitters discarded the idea that a picture is a unique creation.   *peace   the new order   artworks*

contradictoriness Space   *familiar reality familiar reality* Maciunas   trouble *artistic unity* **Schwitters discarded the idea that** ~~a picture is a unique creation.~~   *PEACE* **the new order**   artworks

Now I call myself ~~**MERZ**~~**.   the new order**   unaltered found materials   artworks

pain use anything **Now I call myself** ~~**MERZ**~~**.   the new order**   unaltered found materials *Realism made from real things*   **Art as simple as writing the letter** i.   **the new order**   *Merzbild* paradise Schwitters and Wordsworth lived their last years, died, and are buried--4 miles from each other--in England's Lake District.   *indifferently Merz   familiar reality*

pain   use anything **Now I call myself -MERZ-.**   **the new order**   **the new order**
DO NOT ASK FOR SOULFUL MOODS. *Merz*   *Merzbild* whatever has been taken for
granted ***artistic unity*** *Merzbild*   *Merzbild* use anything to make art   *blatant literal*
presence of objects   **THE DADAIST IS A MIRROR CARRIER.**   *Realism made from*
*real thing*s

paradise Schwitters and Wordsworth lived their last years, died, and are buried--4 miles
from each other--in England's Lake District.   *indifferently Merz*   **Art as simple as**
writing the letter i.   objets trouvés ecstatic *Merz*   *Merzbild* letters pain   use
anything *THE MOST INTERNATIONAL* petit bourgeois *IN THE WORLD.*   **Now I**
call myself -Merz-. **the new order** *familiar reality*

love and hate everything letters dying Maciunas   **A MARVELOUS DILETTANTE**
Realism made from real things   **SCHWITTERS** *avant-garde REFUSE*   *Go out into*
the whole world and make the truth known, the only truth there is, the truth about Anna
Blume.   *Merzbild* **Now I call myself -MERZ-.**   **the new order**   **UNALTERED**
FOUND MATERIALS   *Realism made from real things*   *inchoate experience*

HANNOVER   Why make artworks if you're opposed to art?   *that is correct*   *The*
materials bring into the abstract formal performance a piece of familiar reality.   Schwitters
conventional Fluxus *Realism made from real things* **Now I call myself -MERZ-.**
conventional Fluxus   *The materials bring into the abstract formal performance a piece*
of familiar reality.   *Merzbild* **Now I call myself -MERZ-.**   **the new order**   unaltered
found materials   *Realism made from real things*

19 July 1987
New York

65

11th Merzgedicht in Memoriam *Kurt Schwitters*

writing poems *infinity an art attitude*   A r t i s a u t o n o m o u s .

Merz infinity an art attitude aufgebaut him nonpolitical because he espoused no easily recognized ideology *familiar reality* **love and hate everything** *infinity* **I love and hate everything.**

wooden Huelsenbeck **seriousness** Rumpelstiltskin **seriousness** *familiar reality* **love and hate everything** *infinity* **I love and hate everything.**

wooden antiartistic Huelsenbeck *SCHWITTERS SHIED AWAY.*

love and hate everything *infinity* **A consistent work of art It was not only because they could serve as well as painter's pigment that Schwitters made use of the residues of life, the wretchedest of all materials.**

antiartistic *avant-garde* **Schwitters The Cathedral broke through the ceiling and aspiring upward pushed into Kurt's and Helma's apartment above, leaving one of the rooms with no floor.**

love and hate everything ideology *Tyl Eulenspiegel Tyl Eulenspiegel* **Cage regarded words and letters both as meaningful symbols and as formal design elements writing poems regarded words and letters both as meaningful symbols and as formal design elements** *Combine all branches of art into an artistic unity.*

artworks *familiar reality* *ONE CAN EVEN SHOUT OUT THROUGH REFUSE.*

ONE CAN EVEN SHOUT OUT THROUGH REFUSE.

There is no such thing as inchoate experience.

July - August 1987
New York

12th Merzgedicht in Memoriam Kurt Schwitters

The earlier Merz-drawings look as though the materials composed the collages themselves by virtue of the forces inherent in them.

use anything **lawfully allowed time Hannover strives forward.**

Hannover strives forward.

transcended his conscious abstract-art ideology an active life *The many legible passages are not conducive to reading.*

GESTURES *Blau ist die Farbe Deines gelben Haares.*

close friends found it difficult to reconcile Schwitters *Entartete Kunst* **The Cathedral broke through the ceiling and aspiring upward pushed into Kurt's and Helma's apartment above, leaving one of the rooms with no floor.**

The slogans he composed for display on the municipal trolley line were especially popular.

experience **BUREAUCRATIC REGULATIONS RUBBER-STAMPED MESSAGES When the Germans invaded Norway in 1940, Schwitters escaped with his son to England, where he was interned for the first seventeen months.**

harmonically arranged colored rectangles, the colors, free of painterly modulations, treated as sheer, signatureless, *anonymous* **coats of paint Futurism unaltered found materials** *stupidity of institutions AN IMAGE OF THE REVOLUTION* **Fluxus** *Hollow burns the stomach flame sulfur blood.*

Hülsenbeck excluded Schwitters from the Berlin Club Dada in 1920 because Schwitters was friendly with the Sturm circle and indifferent or opposed to Hülsenbeck's Leninism.

art seems to me injurious to art Syntax gets unhinged.

This was before H.R.H. The Late Duke of Clarence & Avondale.

Now it is a Merzpicture.

Sorry!

Dada a world of violent letter forms Dada a bottle of urine ascribed to Goethe **the last desperate decade of his life** scorned or scoffed at Futurism **the bourgeois world** *stupidity of institutions* **a phonetic sound poem of considerable length with notations of his own devising to indicate rhythm, timing, and emphasis** Johannes Baader **a picture of its creation** *Thus featherbeds are cleaned, dusted, washed, steamed, and dried.*

destroyed by Allied bombs absurd verbal juxtapositions *Die Scheuche* **a phonetic sound poem of considerable length with notations of his own devising to indicate rhythm, timing, and emphasis** a commercial endeavor realizing that Schwitters' artworks function politically *n the early days of* MERZ *his position was anti-functionalist,* purely *artistic: a* ~~*utopian conception*~~.

~~*performer*~~ *Kom***MERZ** *und Privatbank.*

Das Schwein niesst zum Herzen.

~~*geometric simplicity*~~ *Verbürgt rein.*

Schwitters joined visual and verbal, fantastic and mundane, in the *Merzbilder* begun in 1919.

~~*use anything*~~ *graphic designer* penciled images combined with ordinary rubber-stamped messages used on packages to indicate contents, mailing restrictions, or the name and address of the sender never officially joined a Dada group The revolutionary upheaval that followed the armistice provided the break with the culture of the past that was crucial to the development of his idiosyncratic style.

avant-garde Schwitters joined visual and verbal, fantastic and mundane, in the *Merzbilder* begun in 1919.

bring into the abstract formal performance a piece of familiar reality.

Piet Zwart **THE DADAIST IS A MIRROR CARRIER.**

His collages began to lose their constructivist restraints and returned to more open compositions.

After four weeks I was dismissed on the grounds that I was a lazy good-for-nothing.

12 August 1987
New York

13th *Merzgedicht* in Memoriam *Kurt Schwitters*

Pumpfftilffftoo?

Tatlin   Hannah Höch   Berlin   word games
        ALWAYS DO OTHERWISE THAN THE OTHERS.

familiar reality   illusionistic space
            irregular intervals   *stupidity of*
            institutions   **GESTURES**
After the revolution I felt myself free and had to cry
out   my jubilation to the world.

Hannover strives forward   In the early days of
        MERZ *his position was anti-functionalist,* purely
            artistic: ~~a utopian conception~~.

Schwitters's mind and practice roved freely.

    the outbreak of hostilities   *"Die Zoologischer*
                        Garten-Lotterie"
Weisst du es, Anna, weisst du es schon?

Man kann dich auch von hinten lesen und du, du
Herrlichste von allen, du bist von hinten wie von
        vorne
a-n-n-a.

        Word scraps, posterlike, thrown into relief,
        are absorbed directly, optically, penetrating the
unconscious more readily than the conscious, engendering
the   feeling of an oppressive reality.

    Vilmar Huszar   collages   Schwitters
Constructivist ideas of design **Whirl-heap blood's leaf**
        illusionistic familiar reality **Merz ist**

                            form.

Ich werde gegangen
Ich taumeltürme
Welkes windes Blatt
Häuser augen Menschen Klippen
Schmiege Taumel Wind
Menschen steinen Häuser Klippen
Taumeltürme blutes Blatt.

**Schwitters continued to work as an artist through the
last desperate decade of his life.**

wooden   *According to Hülsenbeck, "An Anna Blume"*
lacked aggression and truly deflating irony and was
a product of a taste actually attached to the
most banal bourgeois values and the most
romantic bourgeois sentiments,
even though it also   *mocked them.*

**täglichen aufgebaut wie Kaspar Wordsworth oder
Friedrich Maciunas, Schacko Bluemner**

oder Anna

Blume.

Schwitters's mind and practice roved freely over all the
possibilities available to artists.

streetcar tickets   *I experienced the Revolution*
in the most delightful way and pass for a
Dadaist without being one; as a result,
I could
introduce Dadaism into Holland with complete
impartiality.

Merzbau Hannover, begun by Schwitters around 1923
and continually worked upon for nearly fourteen years,
was twenty years later--five years before his death
--destroyed by Allied bombs.

Blau sengte Flamme Mord sehr ab sehr ab.

THE MOST INTERNATIONAL petit bourgeois *IN THE WORLD.*

watercolors **MIRROR**   streetcar tickets   *FRAGMENTS*
Chicago   theater schedules scorned or scoffed at
**Schwitters' jovial, extrovert, and clownish nature
only concerned with consistency within each work.**

This was before H.R.H. The Late Duke of Clarence
&   Avondale.

Now it is a Merzpicture.

Sorry!

Schoenberg　　Hannover　　Schwitters　**the**
female lavatory of life in a long corridor with
scattered camel dung　　a phonetic sound poem of
considerable length with notations of his own　　　　devising to indicate
rhythm,

　　　　　　　　　　　　　　　　　　　　　　timing,

and　emphasis　　*illusionistic space*　respect,
　like,

　　　　　　　　　　enjoy,
　or be delighted
　Satie　　Moholy-Nagy　　*Suddenly the glorious*
　　　　　　　　　　　　　　　　revolution arrived!

　　　political catchwords　a declaration of love
I am a painter and I nail my pictures together.

Lake　　Hannover　　Cesar Domela　　Hannah Höch
Schlank stachelt Fisch in der Peitscheluft　**MIRROR**
　　　　　　　carefully cropped details from
　　　printers' reject material　Hülsenbeck wrote:
Dada is　　　　　　　　　　*making propaganda against culture.*

small wheels　　Lysaker　　Stein
　　　　　FORTHRIGHTNESS AND GENEROSITY
　　　blatant literal presence of objects
　　　　　　　　　　　Geldig Voor.

　　wire　　*Die Hahnepeter*　　*Weisst du es,*
Anna,　　　　　　　　　　　　*weisst du es schon?*

Man kann dich auch von hinten lesen und du, du
Herrlichste von allen, du bist von hinten wie von
　　　vorne
a-n-n-a.

a commercial endeavor　　avant-garde　　**It is**
　　unimportant　　　　　　*whether or not the*
　　　　　　　material
　　　　　used in a Merzbild was already formed
　　for some　　　　　　*purpose or other.*

a frenzy of rhythmically reeling sentences, sentence
　　　　fragments, words, and　word fragments
Moholy-Nagy
　　There is no such thing as inchoate experience.

allusive possibilities   Hülsenbeck
        thought "An Anna Blume" showed *an idealism made*
            dainty by madness and was rather silly.

Big Love Grotto   *Weisst du es, Anna,*
                    weisst du es schon?

Man kann dich auch von hinten lesen und du, du
Herrlichste von allen, du bist von hinten wie von
            vorne
a-n-n-a.

architecture   **A perambulator wheel, wire netting,**
string, and cotton wool are factors having equal rights
with   paint.

A TRADITIONAL UNDERSTANDING OF ART   *dying*
        odd bits of stationery His collages began
                    to lose their constructivist
restraints and
returned to more open

                        compositions.

a phantasmagoria   torn photographs
            Pumpfftilfftoo?

    The *Merzbau* was *a fabricated monument to the*
     permanence and durability of his
                private, invented
        world, a luminous image, a point of order:
            stasis, a phantasmagoria, a dream grotto.

    In the fourteen years Schwitters worked on the
Merzbau   in Hannover, the edifice grew through the
        ceiling of   the original room,
            broke through the wall of
adjoining   chambers, and descended below the ground
    into a   subterranean cistern.

    As founded by Hugo Ball in Zurich in 1916, Dada
                    sprang from the
same sources as Schwitters' art, stressing the
            instinctive and the
primitive and seeking a secret inner language.

Bevel whirl wind   Cage   fabrics   letters
       painter   desanctification   **Dada**
             pasted scraps of paper
  <u>Der Sturm.</u>

    experience allows her to see them
Schwitters continued to work as an artist through
        the last desperate decade of his life.

Words--their meaning, their sound, their appearance--had
    a central place in all of Schwitters'
    endeavors, as a painter, sculptor, writer,
publisher, performer, lecturer, typographer, and
      graphic designer.

    blatant literal presence of objects   a
commercial endeavor rubber-stamped messages   Weisst du
          es, Anna, weisst du
es schon?

   As the first formation of a serious situation weapons
     obliged everything.

    pasted scraps of paper with a background of
drawn and written motifs indifferently   Schlank
        stachelt Fisch in   *der Peitscheluft*
experience   **love and hate everything**
<u>Geldig Voor.</u>

between his legs he is holding a huge blank cartridge
    Hülsenbeck excluded Schwitters from the Berlin
        Club Dada in 1920 because Schwitters
was   *friendly with the Sturm circle*
and indifferent or   *opposed to Hülsenbeck's*
    Leninism.

  the Karlsruhe *Dammerstock Siedlung Schwitters preferred*
        and was more successful with found
than with   *fabricated elements.*

   The king asked for a drink.

Cesar Domela   *preconstituted*   *Helma Fischer*
  the   **female lavatory of life in a**
        long corridor   **with scattered**
camel   **dung**   *watercolors*
                          disaffection from the
bourgeois world that had   **brought on World**
  War I   Hülsenbeck thought "An   Anna
          Blume" showed *an idealism made*
  dainty by   *madness* and was
               rather silly.

    penciled images combined with ordinary
        rubber-stamped messages used on
          packages to indicate
    contents, mailing restrictions, or the name and
     address of the sender   <u>Geldig</u>   <u>Voor.</u>

  The materials bring into the abstract formal
        performance a piece of familiar
    reality.

  Allgemeines Merz X Programm   watercolors
  Ich taumeltürme   *use anything to make art*   he
        couldn't sleep
           Ambleside
Schwitters believed the deadest language, the most
      outmoded ideas, can generate Weltgefühl
    when they appear suddenly, unexpectedly, in an
entirely unfamiliar setting.

  Art as simple as writing the letter i.

          a point of order: stasis odd
  bits of stationery Huelsenbeck   Raoul Hausmann   Schwitters:
Hülsendadaismus **is politically oriented,**
      against art and against culture: alien
   to *Merz.*

    close friends found it difficult to reconcile
  Schwitters   *wire*   **Remain true to**
               duty, be faithful.

  an extraordinary time   *ONE CAN EVEN SHOUT OUT THROUGH*
    REFUSE, AND THIS IS WHAT I DID, NAILING AND
        GLUING.

advertising design **an extraordinary time**
Braunschweigenmotgeld
writing poems　　*an*　　　　　　　　　　　　　*art*
attitude vandalism **Big Love**
Grotto the Karlsruhe *Dammerstock*　　*Siedlung*
that is correct　THE MOST INTERNATIONAL
petit　　　　　　　　　　　　　　　　　　　bourgeois *IN*
THE WORLD.

*T*HE REVOLUTIONARY UPHEAVAL THAT FOLLOWED THE ARMISTICE
PROVIDED THE BREAK WITH THE
CULTURE OF THE　　　　　　　　　　　　　　　PAST THAT
WAS
CRUCIAL TO THE DEVELOPMENT　　OF HIS IDIOSYNCRATIC STYLE.

~~Madness or a bad joke turns into a solid cultural~~

~~possession~~.

IDIOTIC ADVERTISING SLOGANS　**meine süsse puppe,**
mir ist alles schnuppe,
wenn ich meine schnauze
auf die deine bautze.

ONE CAN EVEN SHOUT OUT THROUGH REFUSE.

Fümms bö wö tää zää uu, Uu see tee wee bee
fümmmmms!

candy wrappers　　**It is unimportant whether or not the**
material used in a *Merzbild* **was already formed**
for　　　　　　**some purpose or other.**

Schlank stachelt Fisch in der Peitscheluft　　**Merz:**
a　　　　　**syllable taken from a bank's letterhead, "Kommerz**
und Privatbank," it carries an aural association
with "abmerzen" ["to reject"], and thus is related
with the abandoned materials Schwitters
resurrected and transformed.

Numbers, meaningless in themselves, suggest the real.

pasted scraps of paper　　Stein
Geldig Voor.

something new from the pieces never culled texts
with　　　　　*cunning ingenuity and*
combined　　　　　　　　*them with intent to*
tease

The Cathedral broke
through the ceiling and aspiring
upward pushed into Kurt's and

Helma's

apartment above, leaving   one
of the rooms   with   no floor.

AN IMAGE OF THE REVOLUTION   O thou, beloved of my
twenty-seven
senses,
I love thine!

the female lavatory of life in a long corridor with
scattered camel dung   *Moon calf*
shines inward   *softly drew bowel fat*
pain softly drew bowel fat   *pain*
softly un-deafened.

(All for the Red Army.)

Apollinaire Chicago aufgebaut   cotton wool
Von der Nationalversammlung Stückwerk.

writer Hülsenbeck wrote: *Dada is making
propaganda against culture.*

Only three lusters has   *the creature bred*
in the glasshouse   **blossomed.**

*Kandinsky   Gefesselter Blick   Entformung,
Eigengift, konsequent,*
Urbegriff.

distancing   Hans Arp an artist's loft
letters   **Blue singed flame murder**
very very down.

*Hans Arp   him nonpolitical because he espoused
no recognized ideology*
the   **tension and**
competitions between parts and
whole *advertising design*
an   **extraordinary**
time   *Braunschweigenmotgeld*
writing poems   *an*   *art*
attitude *vandalism*   **Big Love Grotto**   the
Karlsruhe   *Dammerstock*

Siedlung   that is correct   THE
                          MOST INTERNATIONAL petit bourgeois
                          IN THE
                                                        WORLD.

The revolutionary upheaval that followed the
                          armistice provided the break with the
culture of the   past that was
                 crucial to the development of
                                    his idiosyncratic style.

~~Madness or a bad joke turns into a solid cultural~~
                                    ~~possession~~.

idiotic advertising slogans **meine süsse puppe,**
                                    mir ist alles schnuppe,
                                    wenn ich meine schnauze
                                    auf die deine bautze.

ONE CAN EVEN SHOUT OUT THROUGH REFUSE.

Fümms bö wö tää zää uu, Uu see tee wee bee
fümmmmms!

candy wrappers   **It is unimportant whether or not**
                 the   material used in a *Merzbild* was already
                                    formed for some purpose or other.

Schlank stachelt Fisch in der Peitscheluft   Merz: a
syllable taken from a bank's letterhead, "*Kommerz und*
                 ***Privatbank*," it carries an aural**
                 association with   "*abmerzen*"
["to reject"], and thus is related
                          with the abandoned materials Schwitters
                                    resurrected and
transformed.

Numbers, meaningless in themselves, suggest the real.

a declaration of love   Stein
                 <u>Geldig Voor.</u>

something new from the pieces never culled texts with
          cunning ingenuity and combined them with intent
to   tease **The Cathedral broke through**
                                    the ceiling and aspiring
          upward   pushed into Kurt's and
                 Helma's apartment

                                                                    above,

    leaving one of the rooms with no floor.

AN IMAGE OF THE REVOLUTION
                                                                O thou,

    beloved of my twenty-seven senses,

                                                    I love thine!

the female lavatory of life in a long corridor with
                                    scattered camel dung
*Moon calf shines inward softly drew bowel fat
        pain softly drew bowel fat pain softly
un-deafened.*

                        (All for the Red Army.)

Apollinaire Chicago aufgebaut   cotton wool **Von
                                Der Nationalversammlung**
Stückwerk.

    writer   Hülsenbeck wrote: *Dada is making*
                                            propaganda
    against culture.

Only three lusters has the creature bred in the glasshouse
                                            blossomed.

    *Kandinsky   active in other areas Entformung,
                            Eigengift, konsequent,
        Urbegriff.*

    *distancing   Hans Arp an artist's loft
            letters* **Blue singed flame murder very very**
down.

    theater stubs   *him nonpolitical because he*
    espoused   *no easily recognized ideology*   **the**
        tension and   **competitions between parts**
    and whole *Moon*   *calf shines inward softly*
            drew bowel fat pain softly   *drew bowel fat pain*
softly un-deafened.

    (All for the Red Army.)

    Now I call myself ~~MERZ~~**.**

Experiments are being carried on with white mice
                    which inhabit Merz-pictures specially
                         constructed for the purpose as
well as   *Merz-pictures that will*
restore by   *mechanical means the*
balance disturbed   *by the motions of*
the mice.

     each discarded bit or snippet   **The king asked**
                                              for a drink.

          a subterranean cistern **between his legs he is**
                    holding a huge blank cartridge   *After*
          the   *revolution,*
     I felt myself free and had to cry out
                    my jubilation to the world.

     ideology   *Meaningless elements stand alongside*
                                   "clues," and no
importance is   *attached*
          to decoding.

     The princess winked and ordered that I be
                                        reassembled.

Blau ist die Farbe Deines gelben Haares.

          avant-garde   *playfully embraced every form*
                              of communication
                         Schwitters continued   to work as
an   *artist through the last desperate decade of his life.*

distancing   *I am went* NATURE, FROM THE LATIN
NASCI,   I.E., TO BECOME OR COME INTO BEING,
EVERYTHING   THAT THROUGH ITS OWN
FORCE DEVELOPS, FORMS OR   MOVES.

Dada was ideological without a specific
ideology and purposive
without a purpose, which is why Dada
actions and
objects
could be considered
artistic.

very large collages   Space   Geldfälschung
wird mit Zuchthaus
gestraft!

24 August -- 13 September 1987
New York

14th Merzgedicht in Memoriam Kurt Schwitters

Geldfälschung wird mit Zuchthaus gestraft!

Blau sengte Flamme Mord sehr ab sehr ab.

Meaningless elements stand alongside "clues," and no importance is attached to decoding.

Stein

Architecture todays pays too little attention to the fact that people change a room by their presence.

The princess winked and ordered that I be reassembled.

regarded words and letters both as meaningful symbols and as formal design elements

watercolors

Merzzmalerei makes use not only of paint and canvas, brush and palette, but of all materials perceptible to the eye and of all required implements.

Hülsenbeck wrote: *Dada is making propaganda against culture.*

Blau sengte Flamme Mord sehr ab sehr ab.

Blau sengte Flamme Mord sehr ab sehr ab.

Dada

Dedes nn nn rrrr, ii ee, mpifftillfftoo tilll.

MIRROR

geometric clarity and purity

carefully cropped details from printers' reject material

He disliked my fighting ways, said Hülsenbeck of Schwitters, *and I liked his static, smug middle-class world even less.*

When the Germans invaded Norway in 1940, Schwitters escaped with his son to England, where he was interned for the first seventeen months.

Taumeltürme blutes Blatt

Suddenly the glorious revolution arrived!

Meaningless elements stand alongside "clues," and no importance is attached to decoding.

Meaningless elements stand alongside "clues," and no importance is attached to decoding.

close friends found it difficult to reconcile Schwitters

lecturer

Construction for Noble Ladies.

Braunschweigenmotgeld

Words, sentences, parts of sentences, are cut out of some context and incorporated into a new context.

delighted

Hans Arp

Sinking twists flat together spread askew.

experience allows her to see them

Stein

Stein

Futurism

Menschen steinen Häuser Klippen

use anything to make art

Hülsenbeck excluded Schwitters from the Berlin Club Dada in 1920 because Schwitters was friendly with the Sturm circle and indifferent or opposed to Hülsenbeck's Leninism.

a phonetic sound poem of considerable length with notations of his own devising to indicate rhythm, timing, and emphasis

In the early days of MERZ *his position was anti-functionalist,* purely *artistic:* a utopian conception.

supposedly antiartistic

I experienced the Revolution in the most delightful way and pass for a Dadaist without being one; as a result, I could introduce Dadaism into Holland with complete impartiality.

Apollinaire

Architecture todays pays too little attention to the fact that people change a room by their presence.

Architecture todays pays too little attention to the fact that people change a room by their presence.

There is no such thing as inchoate experience.

probably in New York

A mis- or overprinted page of type was transformed into a work of art by a judicious arrangement of forms around or on top of the rejected material.

Schwitters' theories of advertising design and efforts for the Pelikan company

It is unimportant whether or not the material used in a *Merzbild* was already formed for some purpose or other.

Realism made from real things

told *they imitate nature in its complexity.*

Theo van Doesburg

never officially joined a Dada group

The princess winked and ordered that I be reassembled.

The princess winked and ordered that I be reassembled.

He had no choice but to play the clown.

political

artistic unity

Geldig Voor.

Stempelzeichnungen.

clichés of any kind

Bevel whirl wind

a picture of its creation

aufgebaut

     regarded words and letters both as meaningful symbols and as formal design elements

     regarded words and letters both as meaningful symbols and as formal design elements

clichés

    lecturer

   Laternenpfahl orgelt Küssen breiten Röcke wogen weisse psitzen Kuss.

      I am went
I whirl-heap
Wilted wind's leaf
Houses eyes men cliffs
Bevel whirl wind
Men stone houses cliffs
Whirl-heap blood's leaf

Fluxus

Entformung, Eigengift, konsequent, Urbegriff.

I called it MERZ: *it was a prayer about the victorious end of the war, victorious as once again peace had won in the end; everything had broken down in any case and new things had to be made out of fragments: and this is* ~~MERZ~~.

Weisst du es, Anna, weisst du es schon?
Man kann dich auch von hinten lesen und du, du
Herrlichste von allen, du bist von hinten wie von
        vorne
a-n-n-a.

Johannes Baader

watercolors

watercolors

scraps of newsprint

a phantasmagoria

objets trouvés

an art attitude

as tolerant as possible with respect to its material

"Lautsonate"

an enemy alien

writer

Moon calf shines inward softly drew bowel fat pain softly drew bowel fat pain softly un-deafened. (All for the Red Army.)

Merzzmalerei makes use not only of paint and canvas, brush and palette, but of all materials perceptible to the eye and of all required implements.

Merzzmalerei makes use not only of paint and canvas, brush and palette, but of all materials perceptible to the eye and of all required implements.

antiartistic

Verbürgt rein.

Dadaism as an advertising

artistic unity

Fümms bö wö tää zää uu, Uu see tee wee bee fümmmmms!

glass splinters

a world of violent letter forms

vandalism

Laternenpfahl orgelt Küssen breiten Röcke wogen weisse psitzen Kuss.

Hülsenbeck wrote: *Dada is making propaganda against culture.*

Hülsenbeck wrote: *Dada is making propaganda against culture.*

commitment to art

the new order

mere randomness

reclining emm.

Now it is a Merzpicture. Sorry!

Allgemeines Merz X Programm

playfully embraced every from of communication

Cubism

Liebe Hannah

Blau sengte Flamme Mord sehr ab sehr ab.

Blau sengte Flamme Mord sehr ab sehr ab.

Schwitters: *Hülsendadaismus* **is politically oriented, against art and against culture: alien to *Merz*.**

distancing

There is no such thing as inchoate experience.

logic and grammar

Tzara

Schwitters and Wordsworth lived their last years, died, and are buried--4 miles from each other--in England's Lake District.

Ziiuu ennze ziiuu nnz krr müü, ziiuu ennze ziiuu rinnzkrrmüü; kakete bee bee, rakete bee zee.

A mis- or overprinted page of type was transformed into a work of art by a judicious arrangement of forms around or on top of the rejected material.

Willi Baumeister

Futurism

Futurism

architecture

Heiss fischen Messer schiessen Blut.

The word *Merz* denotes essentially the combination of all conceivable materials for artistic purposes, and technically the principle of equal evaluation of the individual materials.

The *Merzbau was a fabricated monument to the permanence and durability of his private, invented world, a* luminous image, *a point of order: stasis, a phantasmagoria, a dream grotto.*

illusionistic

Schwitters

writing poems
wooden

Schwitters dismissed the importance attached to a picture's individual characteristics as ~~sentimentalism~~.

Pumpfftilfftoo?

Pumpfftilfftoo?

active in other areas

war and exile

89

His collages began to lose their constructivist restraints and returned to more open compositions.

Schwitters' theories of advertising design and efforts for the Pelikan company

The king asked for a drink.

Anna empfing heute in Weimar folgendes aus.

cotton wool

a point of order: stasis

Hannover strives forward

MIRROR

MIRROR

trouble

Komposition

meine süsse puppe,
mir ist alles schnuppe,
wenn ich meine schnauze
auf die deine bautze

People such as Huelsenbeck

Geldfälschung wird mit Zuchthaus gestraft!

20 September 1987
New York

15th Merzgedicht in Memoriam *Kurt Schwitters*

De Stijl Bauhaus the Karlsruhe *Dammerstock Siedlung Mondrian Tatlin Picabia Johannes Baader Constructivist ideas of design Vilmar Huszar Kleine Dada Soirée Die Scheuche Ludwig Hilbersheimer Kate Steinitz a world of violent letter forms a bottle of urine ascribed to Goethe His collages began to lose their constructivist restraints and returned to more open compositions.*

Collages constructivist restraints open compositions never officially joined a Dada group <u>Stempelzeichnungen.</u>

Something new from the pieces penciled images combined with ordinary rubber-stamped messages used on packages to indicate contents, mailing restrictions, or the name and address of the sender The revolutionary upheaval that followed the armistice provided the break with the culture of the past that was crucial to the development of his idiosyncratic style.

Thirteen of his works were confiscated from German museums in 1937 as Degenerate Art.

Rubber-stamped messages Kandinsky Apollinaire Marinetti Cubism.

Clichés of any kind political catchwords bureaucratic regulations worn-out maxims idiotic advertising slogans **a frenzy of rhythmically reeling sentences, sentence fragments, words, and word fragments abrupt reversions to logic** *The princess winked and ordered that I be reassembled.*

Thus featherbeds are cleaned, dusted, washed, steamed, and dried.

Speechless king scared chalk.

Heiss fischen Messer schiessen Blut.

Laternenpfahl orgelt Küssen breiten Röcke wogen weisse psitzen Kuss.

Hotly knives fish shoot blood.

Schlingen Arme breiten Röcke wogen Hals spitzen warme Röheen glatten schlank Füsse Karpfen, Karpfen, Karpfen.

Lamppost strums kisses broad skirts surge white lacework kiss.

Arms twirl broad skirts surge neck sharpen warm pipes smoothe slender legs carps, carps, carps.

The slaughterer jumps forward (This is love), swings club, to lower lower heavy heavy fervently whips to lower heavy heavy very very very very.

Blau sengte Flamme Mord sehr ab sehr ab.

Blue singed flame murder very very down.

Syntax gets unhinged.

Anna empfing heute in Weimar folgendes aus.

Von der Nationalversammlung Stückwerk.

Als erste Bildung einer ernsten Lage Waffen verpflichtete alles.

Anna received today in Weimar the following from.

Before, the National Assembly patchwork.

As the first formation of a serious situation weapons obliged everything.

The many legible passages are not conducive to reading.

The facts of life are not especially interesting to write about: one can't lie, one hasn't experienced anything significant, and yet one lives.

All of us are born too early.

Fümmsböwötääzääuu, pögiff, kwiiee.

Weisst du es, Anna, weisst du es schon?

After the revolution, I felt myself free and had to cry out my jubilation to the world.

Suddenly the glorious revolution arrived!

<u>Das Schwein niesst zum Herzen.</u>

<u>Netzzeichnung.</u>

Everything was destroyed anyway and it was necessary to build something new from the pieces.

Pumpfftilfftoo?

Dedes nn nn rrrr, ii ee, mpifftillffftoo tilll.

Ziiuu ennze ziiuu nnz krr müü, ziiuu ennze ziiuu rinnzkrrmüü; kakete bee bee, rakete bee zee.

Fümms bö wö tää zää uu, Uu see tee wee bee fümmmmms!

Rinnzekete bee bee nnz krr müü ziiuu ennze ziiuu rinnzkrrmüü; rakete bee bee.

After four weeks I was dismissed on the grounds that I was a lazy good-for-nothing.

Since only fools are modest, I am absolutely convinced that I once lived as Rembrandt van Rijn, and I wholeheartedly enjoy the enthusiastic admiration I receive in that guise.

I experienced the Revolution in the most delightful way and pass for a Dadaist without being one; as a result, I could introduce Dadaism into Holland with complete impartiality.

K Merzbild K4 (Bild rot Herz-Kirche).

Merz: a syllable taken from a bank's letterhead, "*Kommerz und Privatbank,*" it carries an aural association with "*abmerzen*" ["to reject"], and thus is related with the abandoned materials Schwitters resurrected and transformed.

Schwitters joined visual and verbal, fantastic and mundane, in the *Merzbilder* begun in 1919.

Braunschweigenmotgeld Geldfälschung wird mit Zuchthaus gestraft!

When the Germans invaded Norway in 1940, Schwitters escaped with his son to England, where he was interned for the first seventeen months.

Entartete Kunst Degenerate Art Schwitters began the *MERZbau* in his house on the Waldhausenstrasse in Hannover in 1920 and worked on it for the next sixteen years.

"*Lautsonate*" Hannah Höch Helma Fischer Raoul Hausmann Theo van Doesburg.

27 September 1987
New York

16th Merzgedicht in Memoriam *Kurt Schwitters*

was.

Kanada,
 forward.

ENTIRELY FOR   *strange wooden*   *the*   them
                 MERZ   *materials.*

indifferently   This   ~~joke~~---*mere presence*
because   large   **I**   *against*   *art*
roved.

<u>*something*</u>   *is.*

was.

performance   **OUT**   and.

<u>This!</u>

<u>reclining.</u>

no.

THE.

<u>Merzpicture.</u>

discarded   ***FORTHRIGHTNESS***   begun
        advertising *experience*   **Elikan.**

forward **Hoppst *too***   or   **could**   <u>Construction.</u>

regarded   <u>for.</u>

collages   ***was.***

Fluxus   *against*   ***ONE***   **and**
antiartistic   upon   petit.

imitate.

AND   ART   **the**   Ambleside   *he*

                                Schwitters'   *Eigengift,*

strives   probably   *Schwitters'*   <u>reclining.</u>

---

28 September 1987
New York

17th Merzgedicht in Memoriam *Kurt Schwitters*

World War I Chicago whatever has been taken for granted whatever has been taken for granted may begin to be qu

es

tione

d an

d

eventually illumined He des

igned posters,
newspaper logos,
theater sc

hedu

les,
and school car

ds for the cities of Hannover and Karlsruhe.

avant-garde Kandinsky playfully emb

raced every fo

rm of commun

ication **On a constantly exp**

anded sculptural/arch

itectural framewo

rk made of wood and plast

er Schwitters applied all the materials that came his way in the co

urse of an act

ive life,
including a bo
ttle of urine ascribed to G

oethe.

Klee *The pr*

incess winked a

nd ordered that I be reassembled.

Elikan merzed a konsequent brocken.

abandoned materials   O thou,
beloved of my twenty-seven senses,
**   I love thine!**

stup

idity of institutions **Speech**

les

s king scared chalk.

REF

USE Als er

ste Bildung einer ernsten Lage Waffen verpflichtete alles.

allusive po

ssibilities Hülsenbeck thought
"An Anna Blum

e"
s

howed
a
n idealism made daint

y by madne

ss and that it was final

1

y rather si

lly.

T

he

big twis

ted-arou

nd child's

he

ad with the syphilitic eyes is warn

ing the embracing couple to be careful.

d

ying Words,

sentenc

es,
parts of sentences,
are cu

t out of some context and incor

porated into a new context.

Welkes windes B

latt   *Ich werde gegangen*
 Ich taumeltürme
  Welkes windes Blatt
 Häuser augen Menschen Klippen
 Schmiege Taumel Wind
 Menschen steinen Häuser Klippen
 Taumeltürme blutes Blatt.

After fo

ur weeks I was dismissed on

the grounds that I was a lazy good-for-nothing.

Elikan merzed a konsequent brocken.

his p

rivate,
invented world cotton wool SOULFUL Wh

y make artwo

rks if you're opposed t

o

art?

The king

asked for a dr

ink.

Surrea

lism rubber-stamp

ed messages disparaged the cult of provocative individualism Vilmar H

us

zar *contradictoriness* Iraq Dates.

Whirl-heap blood's leaf

destr

o

yed by Allied bom

bs

Schwitters preferred a

nd was more successful wit

h found than with fabricate

d el

ements.

man-made hil

l
"Schacko"
Hülsendadai

smus = Husk Dadaism **advert**

ising de

s

ign completed wall Berlin World War II theater schedu

les

Dada was ide

ological without a specific ideology an

d

purpos

ive without a purpose,
whic

h is why Dada actions and objects cou

ld be consider

ed artistic.

Chicago ***Merz ist form.***

geometric clarity and purity *My wet nurse's milk was too thick and there was too little,*
b

ecause she nursed me beyo

n

d the lawfully allowed time.

Merz:
a syllable taken from a bank's letterhead,
"Kommerz und P

rivatbank,"
it carries an aural association with
"abmerzen"
["to reject"],
and th

us is related with the abando

ned mat

erials Schwitters resurrected and transfo

rmed.

transcended his conscious abstract-art ideolog

y *Von der*

Na

tionalversammlung Stückwerk.

Theo van Doesburg Ludwig Hilbersheimer
"Schacko"
p

osters **ART NEEDS CONTEMPLATIVE SELF-ABSORPTION.**

World War II *I am went* advertising design balancing of colors,
forms,
textures,
and typograph

ic fragments

Schwitters represents the brief

time when moder

nism believed itself an instrument o

f social reform.

Cage *Everything was*

destroyed a

nyway and it

was ne

cessary to buil

d something new from the pieces.

contradictoriness a subterranean cistern
"L

autsonate"
Schwi

t

te

rs

represents the brief time when modernism believed itself an instru

ment of s

ocial re

form.

REFUSE posters a poin

t of ord

er:
s

tasis as tolerant as possible with respec

t to its material **Häu**

ser

augen Menschen Klippen *prob*

ably in New Yo

rk Schwitters' expressive power was given

direction by the scrap

s with

which he created fo

rms.

Merzbild Dadaist

*s **The princess winked and o***

rdered that I be reassembled.

<u>Elikan merzed a konsequent brocken.</u>

Dadaists performer <u>Stempelzeichnung</u>

<u>en.</u>

Schwitter

s joined visua

l and verbal,
fantastic and mundane,
in the *Merzbilder* begun in 1919.

Suddenly the glorious revolution arrived!

*dying **Two mushrooms grew eyes stip***

e smooth

bulbs

milk and bored two holes in the king's belly.

The many legible passages are not conducive to reading.

Vordembege-Gildewart **On a constantly expanded sculptural/architectural f**

r

amewo

rk m

ade of wood and plas

ter Schwitters a

pplied all t

he

material

s that came his way in the course of an active l

i

fe,
including a bot

tle

of urine as

cribed to Goethe.

Du!

K Merzbild K4
(Bild rot Herz-Kirche).

Denn in Kanada,
In Amerika
Hopps

t die

klein

e Omama
Immer rinn in d

en Zinnober,
Immer knüppeldicke rinn,
Hopps

t sie unter,
hoppst sie ober,
Mac

ht sie stets den dollsten Zinn.

a frenzy of rhythmically reeling sentences,
sentence fragments,
words,
and word fragments *artworks* Schwitters began the *MERZbau*

in his house on the Waldhausenstr

asse in Hannover in 1920 and worked on it for the next sixteen years.

pasted scraps of paper with a b

ackgro

un

d of drawn and written motifs Hülsenbeck wrote:
Dada is making p

ropaganda against culture.

FRAGMENTS *elements printed from sh*

o

e leat

her and the patterned paper used fo

r wrapping

cakes supposedly antiar

tistic <u>Constructive Composition.</u>

publisher *Der Schlächter s[ringt vor*
(Da

s ist die Liebe),
schwingt Keule senken senken schwer schwer innig p

eitsch

t s

enken schwer schwer sehr sehr sehr sehr.

Schwitters maintained that a reproduction could be as good as an original and painted a number of pictures in more than one copy.

he couldn't sleep vandalism **disaf**

fection fr

o

m

the bourgeois

world tha

t

had brought on World War I include

no antiartistic admixture **I whirl**

-heap Construction for Nobl

e Ladi

es.

an act

ive

life Moon calf shines

inward softly drew bowel fat pain softly drew bowel fat pain softly u

n-deafened.

(All for the Red Army.)

Iraq Dates.

The

"Tran"

texts are the most aggressive and hostile Schwitters ever composed.

Malerei **A MARVELOUS**

DILETTANTE STREETC

AR TICKETS **<u>ART NEEDS CONTEMPLATIVE SELF-ABSORPTION.</u>**

HANS ARP *Threatening or distu*

r

b

ing images are themselves disto

rted through lin

guistic inventiveness.

The *Merzbau was* **a fabricated monument to the p**

ermanence and durability of h

is private,

invented wo

rld,
a **luminous image,**
a point

o

f order:
stasis,
a phantasmag

or

ia,

a dream grotto.

ACTIVE IN OTHER AREAS Ich taumeltürme A DECLARATION OF LOVE Now and then a number,
word,
or p

h

ras

e is written into the picture f

r

eehand.

A co

nsistent work of art *Schwitters' expressive power was given direction by the scraps with which he created form*

s.

Blood rinsed bucket blue ra

y red t

hick whip.

SCORNE

D OR SCOFFED AT *Before,*
the National

Assembl

y patchwork.

SCHWI

T

TE

RS'

**FRIENDS EL LISSITZKY AND THEO VAN DOESBURG CONSIDERED ART A COLLECTIVE ENTERPRISE AND OPPOSED DADA'S PROVOCATIVE INDIVIDUALISM,
AND THEIR VIEWS GREATLY INFLUENCED SCHWITTERS AFTER 1922.**

In memoriam Kurt Schwitters
20 June 1887 -- 8 January 1948
in the month of the fortieth anniversary of his death

21 - 22 January 1988
New York

18th Merzgedicht in Memoriam *Kurt Schwitters*

chwitters was as impo

nt as the fo

rest to the forester.

in a strange c

rtance is attached to decoding.

theater schedu

is

erso

br

ing a pe

n into absolute balanc

oom automatically.

Merz 21.

erstes Veilchen

onpolitical because he espoused no easily r

cognized ideology Near

u on the wall of a barn i

s de

only one to survive war and vandalism--
and now on view at the University of Newcastle.

design design Schwitters joined visual and verb

rzbi

er begun

cessary to

ng new fro

rned or sc

RAGMENTS **logic and grammar abru**

ions

o logic   *Ich werde gegangen*
   Ich taumeltürme
        Welkes windes B

r augen Menschen Kli

en
   chmiege Taumel Wind
   Menschen steinen Häuser Klippen
   Taumeltürme blutes Blatt.

lawfully allo

<u>nsa.</u>

o

rposive without a purpose,

whic

red artistic.

Threatening or distu

ing images

e themselves disto

bout the victor

ious e

nd of the war,
vic

orious as on

on in the end;
ever

case and new things had to be made out of fr

uti

st de

or a Dadaist without b

result,
I

e Dadaism in

co

ner Schwitters preferred and was mo

re suc

ricated elements.

meine süsse pu

ir is

es schnuppe,
wenn ich meine schnauze
auf die deine bautze

Ko

bank.

Schwitter

inue

n artist through the last desperate dec

of his life.

death Han

olutionar

ce pr

ulture of the past that was cruci

s idiosyncratic style.

ons Huelsenb

rawi

een

co

nfiscated fro

rman museums in 1937 as Degenerate Art.

pasted sc

raps of paper Id **Schwitters discarded the idea that** ~~a pie~~
~~tu~~

~~is~~

~~e creation.~~

The slaughterer jumps fo

baut clichés *Dada was ideological without a specific ideology and pur*

ive

ns and objec

ould be con

ost outmoded ideas,
can gener

ctedly,
in an entir

unfami

se

osse Grotte der Lieb

ri

e **bourgeois world** *illusion*

c My wet nurse's milk was to

nursed me beyo

RREGULAR INTERVALS SC

RS' FRIENDS EL LISSITZKY AND THEO VAN DOESBU

IDERED ART A COLLECTIVE ENTERPRIS

E AND OPPOSED DADA'S PRO

bour

is world *The*

no such thing as inc

oate experien

olitically or

cultur

ucti

st re

o more open compositions.

Schwitters dismissed the importance attached to a picture's individual characteristics as ~~sentimentalism~~.

Fümmsb

rshei

er waste materials of modern

ce **Peo**

nbeck pasted scraps o

r c

rt <u>This was before H.R.H. The Late Du</u>

<u>it is</u>

<u>erzpicture.</u>

<u>So</u>

Blut.

Ar
[strophe break between pages]

itte

nt as the forest to the forester.

sc

of n

owed time The *Mer*

cated monument to the per

urabi

s private,

orld,
a luminous image, *a point of order:*
stasis,
a phantasmagoria,
a dream grotto.

Numb

rs, meani

ess in

canvas,
brush and palette,
but o

nd o

required implements.

that is c

rrect **modern German art** Hülsenbeck wrote:
Dada is making propaganda against cu

IRROR *ONE CAN EVEN S*

EFUSE.

Ho

blood.

Str

iving for e

n in a work of art seems to me injurious to art.

USED TRAM TIC

o mushrooms grew eyes stipe smooth bulbs milk an

or

ce in the little bottle of my own ur

uspended.

forward to far.

As founded by Hugo Ball i

sprang from the same

ources as Schwitters' art,
stressing the instinctive and the primitive and seeking a secret inner language.

Marinetti Constructivist ideas of design *b*

ri

e abstract formal performan

ce a piece o

ntic lo

rgeois c

r objects familiar reality.

Now and then a nu

is

en into

br

ics ***Striving for e***

n in a work of art seems to me injurious to art.

only c

on

onsistency *within* each wor

chen Klippen *R*

USE SCHWI

S SHIE

of love made up of word games,
clichés,
and ab

rd verbal juxtaposi

ESS AN

citement bro

n St. Vitus's dance SPACE the Karlsruhe *Dammersto*

R **abrupt reversions to logic**

RU

ILTS

"e"

ABSURD VERBAL JUXTAPO

bulator

ire

**netting, string,
and c**

otton

ool ar

ctor

ual ri

s with paint.

distancing <u>*Ve*</u>

oate experience **DO NOT ASK FOR SOULFUL MOODS.**

**a declaration of love made up of word games,
clichés,**

and ab

rd verbal juxtaposi

e **I love an**

Co

ne all branches o

rt into an artistic

Rinnzekete bee bee nnz krr müü ziiu

iiuu rinnzkrrmüü;
rakete bee bee.

bring into the abs

erfo

bodying a much mor

ie

the tension

co

ns between parts and who

rials   **O thou,**
beloved of my twenty-seven senses,
          I love thine!

The *Merzbau was a fabric*

rmanence and du

ility of his

e,

orld,
a **luminous image,**
a point of order:
stasis,
a phantasmagoria,
a dream grotto.

Anna empfing heute in Weimar folgendes aus.

Entartete Kunst Weisst du es,

Anna,
weisst du es schon?

Man kann dich auch von hinten lesen und du,

du

Herrlichste von allen,

du b

rne

a-n-n-a.

Anna recei

ed today in

c clarity and purity *Als erste Bildung einer ernsten Lage Waffen verpflichtete alles.*

Schwitters' friends El Lissitzky and Theo

n Do

rg c

red art a collective enterprise and opposed Dada's provocative individu

is

eir views greatly influenced Schwitters after 1922.

idio

bottle of ur

ine

nives fish shoot blood.

In memoriam Jackson MacLow (Sr.)
22 January 1888 -- 9 July 1979
on his hundredth birthday

22 January 1988
New York

19th Merzgedicht in Memoriam Kurt Schwitters

active in other areas never culled texts with cunning ingenuity and combined them with intent to tease **the bourgeois world** vandalism *Words--their meaning, their sound, their appearance--had a central place in all of Schwitters' endeavors, as a painter, sculptor, writer, publisher, performer,*

lecturer,

typographer, ordered

Elikan merzed

fragments gather

paradise of art's *Urbegriff* **Whirl-heap**

blood's leaf

abrupt reversions to logic Rumpelstiltskin Marinetti Constructivist ideas of design In *Arbeiterbild* red headlinelike

letters produce the effect of a revolutionary signal, an incitement to rebellion.
After the

and had to cry out my jubilation

world.
writer clichés of any kind letters Braunschweigenmotgeld **Merz: a syllable**

from a bank's letterhead, "*Kommerz und*

carries an

association with "*abmerzen***" ["to reject"], and thus is related**

abandoned materials Schwitters resurrected

collages began to lose their

restraints and returned to more open compositions.
By his very nature he was Dada.
logic

and grammar *Anna empfing*

in Weimar

folgendes aus.
Schwitters

began the *MERZbau*

house on

the Waldhausenstrasse in Hannover in 1920 and worked on it for the next sixteen years.
transcended his conscious abstract-art ideology

were an

impoverished country, I had to cry out my jubilation to the world economically, using what I could find.
cropped

from printers' reject material **GESTURES** *Stein* **Schwitters** Whirl-heap blood's leaf

advertising the
pohplaslan
p
end of all Constructivist ideas of design *excitement* **disaffection from the**

that had brought on

World War I *His* lifework *was never finished.*
antiartistic *Striving for expression in a work of art*
seems to me injurious to art.
forward to far.
In the early

of MERZ *his position was anti-functionalist,*

artistic: a

~~utopian conception~~.
Fümms bö wö tää zää uu, Uu see tee wee bee fümmmmms!
desanctification odd bits of stationery smooth biomorphic forms Chanson des autres is i.
love

and hate everything *I wonder whether one might not construct*

weights to bring a person into absolute balance with

a room automatically.
Blood rinsed bucket blue ray red thick whip.
whatever has been taken for granted

may begin

questioned and

SOULFUL *experience Geldfälschung wird mit Zuchthaus*

gestraft!
Schwitters

house on

the Waldhausenstrasse in Hannover in 1920 and worked on it for the next sixteen years.
pasted scraps of paper   **O thou, beloved of my twenty-seven senses,**
                                      I love thine!

Hülsenbeck excluded Schwitters from the Berlin Club Dada in 1920 because Schwitters
was friendly with the Sturm circle and indifferent or opposed to Hülsenbeck's Leninism.
graphic

designer **It is unimportant**

used in a *Merzbild* **was already formed for some purpose**

or other.
The Nazis invaded Norway in 1940.
Fluxus

stabs fish

the whipair

dance **Schwitters maintained**

**reproduction could be as good as an original and painted a number of pictures in more
than one copy.**

produce the effect of a revolutionary

incitement to rebellion.
On a

constantly expanded sculptural/architectural

**framework made of wood and plaster Schwitters applied all the materials that came his
way in the course**

including a bottle of urine ascribed to Goethe.

aufgebaut absurd verbal juxtapositions In the fourteen years
Schwitters worked on the *Merzbau* in Hannover, the edifice grew

original room, broke through the wall of adjoining

and descended below the ground into a subterranean cistern.

23 January 1988
New York

20th Merzgedicht in Memoriam Kurt Schwitters

and for the Saint Marks Poetry Project

Schwitters' jovial, clownish nature fragment*ed* Helma's apartment floor.

Pelikan sleekly in the whipair's **jovial, extrovert nature** *experienced* New York, **perceived released from objects' mundane functions.**

Disaffection had *THIS NAILING too.*

Bussum's *featherbeds are* Pelikan's scraps experience allows her to letter with ingenuity.

Newsprint forms a world of **objects reduced to romantic cartridges.**

Bourgeois BLANK DADAISTS consume texts combined by Pelikan's **MIRROR Kate Steinitz sleeps on and loves** to tease.

Couldn't A CARRIER's *unity* cull *political catchwords?*

Violent *jubilation freed* the *cry,* **as the revolution suddenly arrived!**

I never *felt my* **vandalism** *world.*

Klee **IS** ~~utopian~~.

FORTHRIGHTNESS AND GENEROSITY **commit*t*ed Schwitters** *to cry***ing.**

A complete theory embodying *jubilation delighted* **Schwitters.**

Stein opposed revolutionary incitement.

Apollinaire printed fragments of *artworks* **rhythmically.**

Klee **sentenced** *pictures to* **design patterned** rebellion, **unexpectedly** *possible, free, tolerant* **in** *jubilation.*

The revolution **was** *not especially interesting.*

26 - 28 January 1988
New York

21st Merzgedicht in Memoriam *Kurt Schwitters*

Clichés spontaneously encountered a world of violent letter forms **when close friends found it difficult to reconcile Schwitters** to labels after thirteen of his works were confiscated from German museums in 1937 as Degenerate Art.

Ludwig Hilbersheimer labeled a subterranean cistern *fantastic* though *by his very nature he was Dada.*

In paradise avant-garde school card numbers, meaningless in themselves, suggest the real.

A declaration of love made up of word games, clichés, and absurd verbal juxtapositions **served as well as painter's pigment when Schwitters made use of the residues of life, the wretchedest of all materials.**

<u>Now it is a Merzpicture.</u>

In the geometric simplicity of ***Ziiuu ennze ziiuu nnz krr müü, ziiuu ennze ziiuu rinnzkrrmüü; kakete bee bee, rakete bee zee*** the unreal quality of inflation has been evoked.

Gathered into the paradise of art, Schoenberg, Marinetti, and **the end of all the familiar materials of everyday life could be perceived as independent aesthetic objects released from their mundane functions.**

Abandoned materials transcended his conscious abstract-art ideology.

Moholy-Nagy, *after the revolution, felt himself free and had to cry out his jubilation to the world.*

Klee necessarily built something new from the fragments of ***art's*** allusive possibilities.

Schwitters continually worked upon *Merzbau Hannover* for nearly fourteen years.

Close friends found it difficult to reconcile *me to injurious art.*

7 February 1988
New York

22nd Merzgedicht in Memoriam Kurt Schwitters

{ *see pp. 212 ff. for performance text, instructions, and musical notation* }

Schwitters maintained that a reproduction could love and hate everything.

Be as good as an original and paint a number of open compositions **in more than one copy.**

Since only fools are modest, I am absolutely convinced that Nazis invaded Norway in 1940.

I once lived as Rembrandt van Rijn, and I wholeheartedly enjoy illusionistic space.

Merzbau Hannover **pictured** a declaration of ecstatic love *I receive in that guise.*

I experienced enthusiastic admiration in the most delightful way with complete impartiality.

Dadaism passes for a Revolution without being one; as a result, I could introduce pasted scraps of paper *into Holland.*

The *Dadaist* used tram tickets and stamps, odd bits of stationery, torn photographs, wood, wire, fabric, small wheels, candy wrappers, labels, glass splinters, Space, clichés, Maciunas, etc.

Dedes nn nn rrrr, ii ee, mpifftillfftoo tilll.

Hülsenbeck, later a Jungian shrink in New York, was a Leninist cornball with a background of *REFUSE and* drawn and written motifs in Berlin.

He disliked Schwitters, *and I liked his smug fighting middle-class ways & world even less.*

Schwitters made use of the residues of the wretchedest delight **as well as painter's pigment** to build something new.

It was only because A MARVELOUS DILETTANTE said *Rinnzekete bee bee nnz krr müü ziiuu ennze ziiuu rinnzkrrmüü; rakete bee bee* **that** he **could serve life.**

Schwitters *carefully cropped* Hülsenbeck's *rejected* fragments of serious **commitment to art** from **all** necessary **material** *details.*

Kleine <u>*reine*</u> *Dada Soirée.*

Since a pure image maker *lived as Rembrandt van Rijn, I wholeheartedly enjoy* **geometric clarity and purity.**

I am absolutely convinced that only fools are small wheels.

Before *my Kleine Dada Soirée* he couldn't sleep *in that illusionistic space.*

Once chagrined *and modest, I receive enthusiastic admiration from printers.*

February - March 1988
New York

23rd *Merzgedicht* in Memoriam *Kurt Schwitters*

Geldig Voor.

Hülsenbeck, later a Jungian shrink in New York, was a Leninist cornball in Berlin.

World War I *Hotly knives fish shoot blood.*

Die Märchen vom Paradies Kleine Dada Soirée Braunschweigenmotgeld **Menschen steinen Häuser Klippen Welkes windes Blatt** *Everything was destroyed anyway and it was necessary to build something new from the pieces.*

The unreal quality of the inflation of **geometric clarity and purity** has been evoked.

The princess Helma Fischer *winked and ordered that I be reassembled.*

Nächtlichhes Dorf.

Schlingen Arme breiten Röcke wogen Hals spitzen warme Röheen glatten schlank Füsse Karpfen, Karpfen, Karpfen.

Weisst Du es, Anna, weisst Du es schon? Man kann Dich auch von hinten lesen und Du, Du Horrlichste von allen, Du bist von hinten wie von vorne: A--------N--------N--------A.

His **lifework** *was never finished.*

After four weeks I was dismissed on the grounds that I was a lazy good-for-nothing.

Architecture todays pays too little attention to the fact that people change a room by their presence.

The Merzbarn evoked the wonder of a natural curiosity.

"*Lautsonate*" Der Sturm.

Everything was destroyed anyway and it was necessary to build something new from the pieces.

Spontaneous encounters **Schwiege Taumel Wind** *Gefesselter Blick* When Hülsenbeck wrote about Club Dada, *You can join without commitments,* he meant, *You can join only without any other commitments.*

A new philosophy of social utility Constructive Composition.

2 June 1988
New York

24th *Merzgedicht* in Memoriam *Kurt Schwitters*

love and hate everything writing poems regarded words and letters both as meaningful symbols and as formal design elements Walter Gropius everyday-language banalities *His lifework was never finished.*

love and hate everything supposedly antiartistic *The facts of life are not especially interesting to write about: one can't lie, one hasn't experienced anything significant, and yet one lives.*

love and hate everything De Stijl clichés of any kind Schwitters *Tyll Eulenspiegel All of us are born too early.*

love and hate everything Bauhaus political catchwords antiartistic *mere* randomness *Fümmsböwötääzääuu, pögiff, kwiiee.*

love and hate everything the Karlsruhe *Dammerstock Siedlung* bureaucratic regulations *blatant literal presence of objects* use anything to make art *Weisst du es, Anna, weisst du es schon?*

love and hate everything Mondrian worn-out maxims distancing **difficult to reconcile** *After the revolution, I felt myself free and had to cry out my jubilation to the world.*

love and hate everything Tatlin idiotic advertising slogans *familiar reality* A TRADITIONAL UNDERSTANDING OF ART *Suddenly the glorious revolution arrived!*

love and hate everything Picabia **a frenzy of rhythmically reeling sentences, sentence fragments, words, and word fragments seriousness** *REFUSE* Das Schwein niesst zum Herzen.

love and hate everything Johannes Baader **abrupt reversions to logic** Hannover **SOULFUL** Netzzeichnung.

love and hate everything Constructivist ideas of design *The princess winked and ordered that I be reassembled.*

love and hate everything commitment to art Dadaism as an advertising *Everything was destroyed anyway and it was necessary to build something new from the pieces.*

love and hate everything Vilmar Huszar *Thus featherbeds are cleaned, dusted, washed, steamed, and dried.*

love and hate everything continually worked upon for nearly fourteen years *Pumpfftilffftoo?*

love and hate everything *Kleine Dada Soirée Speechless king scared chalk.*

love and hate everything *infinity Dedes nn nn rrrr, ii ee, mpifftillfftoo tilll.*

love and hate everything *Die Scheuche Heiss fischen Messer schiessen Blut.*

love and hate everything preconstituted A r t i s a u t o n o m o u s.

love and hate everything *Ziiuu ennze ziiuu nnz krr müü, ziiuu ennze ziiuu rinnzkrrmüü; kakete bee bee, rakete bee zee.*

love and hate everything Ludwig Hilbersheimer *Laternenpfahl orgelt Küssen breiten Röcke wogen weisse psitzen Kuss.*

love and hate everything letters **I love and hate everything.**

love and hate everything *Fümms bö wö tää zää uu, Uu see tee wee bee fümmmmms!*

love and hate everything Kate Steinitz *Hotly knives fish shoot blood.*

love and hate everything *Striving for expression in a work of art seems to me injurious to art.*

love and hate everything *Entformung, Eigengift, konsequent, Urbegriff.*

love and hate everything *Rinnzekete bee bee nnz krr müü ziiuu ennze ziiuu rinnzkrrmüü; rakete bee bee.*

love and hate everything a world of violent letter forms *Schlingen Arme breiten Röcke wogen Hals spitzen warme Röheen glatten schlank Füsse Karpfen, Karpfen, Karpfen.*

love and hate everything *THE MOST INTERNATIONAL* petit bourgeois *IN THE WORLD.*

love and hate everything very large collages *After four weeks I was dismissed on the grounds that I was a lazy good-for-nothing.*

love and hate everything a bottle of urine ascribed to Goethe *Lamppost strums kisses broad skirts surge white lacework kiss.*

love and hate everything whatever has been taken for granted discarded unfinished pages *Since only fools are modest, I am absolutely convinced that I once lived as Rembrandt van Rijn, and I wholeheartedly enjoy the enthusiastic admiration I receive in that guise.*

love and hate everything In the fourteen years Schwitters worked on the *Merzbau* in Hannover, the edifice grew through the ceiling of the original room, broke through the wall of adjoining chambers, and descended below the ground into a subterranean cistern.

love and hate everything *Arms twirl broad skirts surge neck sharpen warm pipes smoothe slender legs carps, carps, carps.*

love and hate everything *FORTHRIGHTNESS AND GENEROSITY* paradise *I experienced the Revolution in the most delightful way and pass for a Dadaist without being one; as a result, I could introduce Dadaism into Holland with complete impartiality.*

love and hate everything His collages began to lose their constructivist restraints and returned to more open compositions.

love and hate everything *Der Schlächter s[ringt vor (Das ist die Liebe), schwingt Keule senken senken schwer schwer innig peitscht senken schwer schwer sehr sehr sehr sehr.*

love and hate everything *experience* A **consistent work of art** K Merzbild K4 (Bild rot Herz-Kirche).

love and hate everything collages *The slaughterer jumps forward (This is love), swings club, to lower lower heavy heavy fervently whips to lower heavy heavy very very very very.*

love and hate everything a pure image maker Chicago **Merz: a syllable taken from a bank's letterhead, "*Kommerz und Privatbank*," it carries an aural association with "*abmerzen*" ["to reject"], and thus is related with the abandoned materials Schwitters resurrected and transformed.**

love and hate everything constructivist restraints *Blau sengte Flamme Mord sehr ab sehr ab.*

love and hate everything Cage *Malerei* Schwitters joined visual and verbal, fantastic and mundane, in the *Merzbilder* begun in 1919.

love and hate everything open compositions *Blue singed flame murder very very down.*

love and hate everything *Combine all branches of art into an artistic unity.*

love and hate everything Du!

love and hate everything *Braunschweigenmotgeld* never officially joined a Dada group *Syntax gets unhinged.*

love and hate everything ecstatic avant-garde *Geldfälschung wird mit Zuchthaus gestraft!*

love and hate everything Stempelzeichnungen.

love and hate everything *Anna empfing heute in Weimar folgendes aus.*

love and hate everything *fantastic* death **When the Germans invaded Norway in 1940, Schwitters escaped with his son to England, where he was interned for the first seventeen months.**

love and hate everything something new from the pieces *Von der Nationalversammlung Stückwerk.*

love and hate everything *Hannover strives forward Komposition Entartete Kunst* penciled images combined with ordinary rubber-stamped messages used on packages to indicate contents, mailing restrictions, or the name and address of the sender *Als erste Bildung einer ernsten Lage Waffen verpflichtete alles.*

love and hate everything *illusionistic* desanctification Degenerate Art The revolutionary upheaval that followed the armistice provided the break with the culture of the past that was crucial to the development of his idiosyncratic style.

love and hate everything *Anna received today in Weimar the following from.*

love and hate everything *Merz* Lake Schwitters began the *MERZbau* in his house on the Waldhausenstrasse in Hannover in 1920 and worked on it for the next sixteen years.

love and hate everything Thirteen of his works were confiscated from German museums in 1937 as Degenerate Art.

love and hate everything *Before, the National Assembly patchwork.*

love and hate everything him nonpolitical because he espoused no easily recognized ideology *aufgebaut "Lautsonate"* rubber-stamped messages *As the first formation of a serious situation weapons obliged everything.*

love and hate everything praxis beginning Hannah Höch Kandinsky *The many legible passages are not conducive to reading.*

love and hate everything *REFUSE Kom***MERZ** *und Privatbank.*

love and hate everything Apollinaire *Meaningless elements stand alongside "clues," and no importance is attached to decoding.*

love and hate everything Space Tzara Raoul Hausmann Marinetti *Word scraps, posterlike, thrown into relief, are absorbed directly, optically, penetrating the unconscious more readily than the conscious, engendering the feeling of an oppressive reality.*

love and hate everything use anything pain Theo van Doesburg Cubism scraps of newsprint avant-garde sleep Hans Arp Futurism theater stubs **The Cathedral broke through the ceiling and aspiring upward pushed into Kurt's and Helma's apartment above, leaving one of the rooms with no floor.**

love and hate everything completed wall *"An Anna Blume"* Dada streetcar tickets conventional Dadaists Hülsenbeck excluded Schwitters from the Berlin Club Dada in 1920 because Schwitters was friendly with the Sturm circle and indifferent or opposed to Hülsenbeck's Leninism.

love and hate everything Dresden Numbers, meaningless in themselves, suggest the real.

love and hate everything each discarded bit or snippet Ambleside Hülsenbeck, later a Jungian shrink in New York, was a Leninist cornball in Berlin.

love and hate everything Berlin never culled texts with cunning ingenuity and combined them with intent to tease <u>Construction for Noble Ladies.</u>

love and hate everything he couldn't sleep <u>Bussum, Bussum, Bussum.</u>

love and hate everything the outbreak of hostilities In <u>*Arbeiterbild*</u> red headlinelike letters produce the effect of a revolutionary signal, an incitement to rebellion.

love and hate everything Huelsenbeck *wooden* <u>Der Sturm.</u>

love and hate everything Words--their meaning, their sound, their appearance--had a central place in all of Schwitters' endeavors, as a painter, sculptor, writer, publisher, performer, lecturer, typographer, and graphic designer.

love and hate everything Now and then a number, word, or phrase is written into the picture freehand.

love and hate everything *imitating nature in its manner of operation* Lysaker <u>Nächtlichhes Dorf.</u>

love and hate everything painter *I wonder whether one might not construct a system of weights to bring a person into absolute balance with a room automatically.*

love and hate everything Maciunas dying El Lissitzky sculptor *Architecture todays pays too little attention to the fact that people change a room by their presence.*

love and hate everything the most banal detritus told *they imitate nature in its complexity.*

love and hate everything Schwitters' friends El Lissitzky and Theo van Doesburg considered art a collective enterprise and opposed Dada's provocative individualism, and their views greatly influenced Schwitters after 1922.

love and hate everything writer *Experiments are being carried on with white mice which inhabit Merz-pictures specially constructed for the purpose as well as Merz-pictures that will restore by mechanical means the balance disturbed by the motions of the mice.*

love and hate everything *stupidity of institutions* **close friends found it difficult to reconcile Schwitters** *Allgemeines Merz X Programm* **publisher** *The earlier Merz-drawings look as though the materials composed the collages themselves* by virtue of the forces inherent in them.

love and hate everything in a strange context **täglichen aufgebaut wie Kaspar Wordsworth oder Friedrich Maciunas, Schacko Bluemner oder Anna Blume.**

love and hate everything Schwitters's mind and practice roved freely over all the possibilities available to artists.

love and hate everything *Gefesselter Blick* performer *grosse Grotte der Liebe* experience allows her to see them only concerned with consistency *within* each work.

love and hate everything <u>Geldig Voor.</u>

love and hate everything Big Love Grotto THE DADAIST IS A MIRROR CARRIER.

love and hate everything *Schwitters' method is that of Realism made from real things.*

love and hate everything *Weisst du es, Anna, weisst du es schon?*

love and hate everything *Man kann dich auch von hinten lesen und du, du Herrlichste von allen, du bist von hinten wie von vorne a-n-n-a.*

love and hate everything typographer **the female lavatory of life in a long corridor with scattered camel dung** destroyed by Allied bombs *bring into the abstract formal performance a piece of familiar reality.*

love and hate everything allusive possibilities graphic designer **between his legs he is holding a huge blank cartridge** *Realism made from real things Such political convictions as he had were more against than for--against war, against the stupidity of institutions.*

love and hate everything active in other areas modern German art **The big twisted-around child's head with the syphilitic eyes is warning the embracing couple to be careful.**

love and hate everything *There is no such thing as inchoate experience.*

love and hate everything Fluxus *forward to far.*

love and hate everything abandoned materials <u>Für Bieling.</u>

love and hate everything The *soul* **of the work was much more important than its visible aspects.**

love and hate everything *Dada was ideological without a specific ideology and purposive without a purpose, which is why Dada actions and objects could be considered artistic.*

love and hate everything <u>***ALWAYS DO OTHERWISE THAN THE OTHERS.***</u>

love and hate everything The familiar materials of everyday life could be perceived as independent aesthetic objects released from their mundane functions.

love and hate everything disaffection from the bourgeois world that had brought on World War I The word *Merz* denotes essentially the combination of all conceivable materials for artistic purposes, and technically the principle of equal evaluation of the individual materials.

love and hate everything *smooth biomorphic forms* <u>reclining emm.</u>

love and hate everything balancing of colors, forms, textures, and typographic fragments **the bourgeois world** *Merzzmalerei* **makes use not only of paint and canvas, brush and palette, but of all materials perceptible to the eye and of all required implements.**

love and hate everything *illusionistic space* probably in New York necessary to build something new from the fragments World War I **It is unimportant whether or not the material used in a** *Merzbild* **was already formed for some purpose or other.**

love and hate everything objets trouvés *meine süsse puppe, mir ist alles schnuppe, wenn ich meine schnauze auf die deine bautze* geometric simplicity World War II **A perambulator wheel, wire netting, string, and cotton wool are factors having equal rights with paint.**

love and hate everything a picture of its creation <u>ART NEEDS CONTEMPLATIVE SELF-ABSORPTION.</u>

love and hate everything A mis- or overprinted page of type was transformed into a work of art by a judicious arrangement of forms around or on top of the rejected material.

love and hate everything Schwitters' theories of advertising design and efforts for the Pelikan company *Hülsendadaismus = Husk Dadaism* chagrined gather them into the paradise of art's *Urbegriff* used tram tickets and stamps advertising design *Schwitters preferred and was more successful with found than with fabricated elements.*

love and hate everything *complexity* <u>This was before H.R.H. The Late Duke of Clarence & Avondale.</u>

love and hate everything <u>Now it is a Merzpicture.</u>

love and hate everything <u>Sorry!</u>

love and hate everything odd bits of stationery Pelikan wire netting **the new order Now I call myself ~~MERZ.~~**

love and hate everything torn photographs **the last desperate decade of his life** cotton wool *<u>Verbürgt rein.</u>*

love and hate everything Schwitters' jovial, extrovert, and clownish nature wood **The slogans he composed for display on the municipal trolley line were especially popular.**

love and hate everything Hülsenbeck thought "An Anna Blume" showed *an idealism made dainty by madness* and that it was finally *rather silly.*

love and hate everything **MIRROR** transcended his conscious abstract-art ideology wire *Ursonate According to Hülsenbeck, "An Anna Blume" lacked aggression and truly deflating irony and was a product of a taste actually attached to the most banal bourgeois values and the most romantic bourgeois sentiments, even though it also mocked them.*

love and hate everything *Merzbau Hannover* **the tension and competitions between parts and whole** fabrics **a phonetic sound poem of considerable length with notations of his own devising to indicate rhythm, timing, and emphasis** reduce romantic love to a bourgeois consumer object *inchoate experience* embodying a much more complete theory pasted scraps of paper The Nazis invaded Norway in 1940.

love and hate everything *He disliked my fighting ways,* said Hülsenbeck of Schwitters, *and I liked his static, smug middle-class world even less.*

love and hate everything *Merzbild* *artistic unity* small wheels **On a constantly expanded sculptural/architectural framework made of wood and plaster Schwitters applied all the materials that came his way in the course of an active life, including a bottle of urine ascribed to Goethe.**

love and hate everything Hülsenbeck wrote: *Dada is making propaganda against culture.*

love and hate everything **DO NOT ASK FOR SOULFUL MOODS.**

love and hate everything Schwitters's mind and practice roved freely.

love and hate everything candy wrappers an active life Schwitters: *Hülsendadaismus* **is politically oriented, against art and against culture: alien to** *Merz.*

love and hate everything Schwitters whatever has been taken for granted may begin to be questioned and eventually illumined labels vandalism *Hülsendadaismus = Husk Dadaism* unaltered found materials realizing that Schwitters' artworks function politically glass splinters a subterranean cistern *I was a Dadaist without intending to be one.*

love and hate everything Art as simple as writing the letter i.

love and hate everything *art seems to me injurious to art pasted scraps of paper with a background of drawn and written motifs* Surrealism *Ich werde gegangen* artworks *totally disabled* waste materials of modern life a new philosophy of social utility **Ich taumeltürme** *Chanson des autres is i.*

love and hate everything *lawfully allowed time* pasted scraps of paper with a background of drawn and written motifs, used tram tickets and stamps, odd bits of stationery, torn photographs, wood, wire, fabric, small wheels, candy wrappers, labels, glass splinters, etc.

love and hate everything an extraordinary time Welkes windes Blatt delighted *"Natural"* *materials bring into the picture the contingency and fluidity of a reality other than the pictorial.*

love and hate everything <u>Constructive Composition.</u>

love and hate everything *After the revolution I felt myself free and had to cry out my jubilation to the world.*

love and hate everything Häuser augen Menschen Klippen *excitement brought on St. Vitus's dance as tolerant as possible with respect to its material* a declaration of love made up of word games, clichés, and absurd verbal juxtapositions *Since we were an impoverished country, I had to cry out my jubliation to the world economically, using what I could find.*

love and hate everything Schwiege Taumel Wind GESTURES ~~Madness or a bad joke turns into a solid cultural possession~~.

love and hate everything a declaration of love watercolors **Menschen steinen Häuser Klippen** Id <u>**AVOID: BECOMING THE CLASSICS OF TOMORROW.**</u>

love and hate everything word games drawings **Taumeltürme blutes Blatt** *indifferently* Schwitters and Wordsworth lived their last years, died, and are buried--4 miles from each other--in England's Lake District.

love and hate everything clichés architecture *Ich werde gegangen* **Ich taumeltürme Welkes windes Blatt Häuser augen Menschen Klippen Schmiege Taumel Wind Menschen steinen Häuser Klippen Taumeltürme blutes Blatt.**

love and hate everything *man-made hill* **Schwitters maintained that a reproduction could be as good as an original and painted a number of pictures in more than one copy.**

love and hate everything absurd verbal juxtapositions design *I am went ONE CAN EVEN SHOUT OUT THROUGH REFUSE.*

love and hate everything Schwitters dismissed the importance attached to a picture's individual characteristics as ~~sentimentalism~~.

love and hate everything elements printed from shoe leather and the patterned paper used for wrapping cakes typography **I whirl-heap *PEACE* Schwitters discarded the idea that** ~~a picture is a unique creation~~.

love and hate everything The unreal quality of the inflation has been evoked.

love and hate everything *Liebe Hannah* **Wilted wind's leaf** Rumpelstiltskin *Hannover strives forward.*

love and hate everything disparaged the cult of provocative individualism **a new geometric simplicity Houses eyes men cliffs** *SCHWITTERS SHIED AWAY.*

love and hate everything *By his very nature he was Dada.*

love and hate everything settled in Lysaker, Norway, not far from Oslo, and began a second *Merzbau* **declared his personal independence Bevel whirl wind** *that is correct My wet nurse's milk was too thick and there was too little, because she nursed me beyond the lawfully allowed time.*

love and hate everything Near Ambleside, in the Lake District, he began a third *Merzbau* on the wall of a barn in Little Langdale, incomplete at his death in 1948--the only one to survive war and vandalism--and now on view at the University of Newcastle.

love and hate everything a commercial endeavor **Men stone houses cliffs** *political I called it* MERZ: *it was a prayer about the victorious end of the war, victorious as once again peace had won in the end; everything had broken down in any case and new things had to be made out of fragments: and this is* ~~MERZ~~.

love and hate everything Schwitters represents the brief time when modernism believed itself an instrument of social reform.

love and hate everything irregular intervals **Whirl-heap blood's leaf** *against war carefully cropped details from printers' reject material* <u>Hansa.</u>

love and hate everything geometric clarity and purity *I am went* **I whirl-heap Wilted wind's leaf Houses eyes men cliffs Bevel whirl wind Men stone houses cliffs Whirl-heap blood's leaf** *AN IMAGE OF THE REVOLUTION* **Schwitters reveals himself as** ~~a naive utopian~~.

love and hate everything <u>Fossil.</u>

love and hate everything The "Tran" texts are the most aggressive and hostile Schwitters ever composed.

love and hate everything To the Berlin Dada group the Sturm group symbolized what was bankrupt in German art.

love and hate everything *FRAGMENTS In the early days of* MERZ *his position was anti-functionalist,* purely *artistic:* ~~a utopian conception~~.

love and hate everything war and exile *Die Hahnepeter As founded by Hugo Ball in Zurich in 1916, Dada sprang from the same sources as Schwitters' art, stressing the instinctive and the primitive and seeking a secret inner language.*

love and hate everything *ONE CAN EVEN SHOUT OUT THROUGH REFUSE, AND THIS IS WHAT I DID, NAILING AND GLUING.*

love and hate everything NATURE, FROM THE LATIN NASCI, I.E., TO BECOME OR COME INTO BEING, EVERYTHING THAT THROUGH ITS OWN FORCE DEVELOPS, FORMS OR MOVES.

love and hate everything interned as an enemy alien *Die Märchen vom Paradies I am a painter and I nail my pictures together.*

love and hate everything Elikan merzed a konsequent brocken.

love and hate everything *Blau ist die Farbe Deines gelben Haares.*

love and hate everything an enemy alien <u>*Merz 21. erstes Veilchenheft.*</u>

love and hate everything *Art to Schwitters was as important as the forest to the forester.*

love and hate everything *excitement Rot is die Farbe Deines grünen Vogels.*

love and hate everything spontaneous encounters "*Die Zoologischer Garten*-Lotterie" When Hülsenbeck wrote about Club Dada, *You can join without commitments,* he meant, *You can join only without any other commitments.*

love and hate everything *The materials bring into the abstract formal performance a piece of familiar reality.*

love and hate everything *Denn in Kanada, In Amerika Hoppst die kleine Omama Immer rinn in den Zinnober, Immer knüppeldicke rinn, Hoppst sie unter, hoppst sie ober, Macht sie stets den dollsten Zinn.*

love and hate everything playfully embraced every form of communication "*Schacko*" Schwitters' application to join Club Dada was rejected.

love and hate everything Why make artworks if you're opposed to art?

love and hate everything *Schwitters' expressive power was given direction by the scraps with which he created forms.*

love and hate everything Vordembege-Gildewart *Blood rinsed bucket blue ray red thick whip.*

love and hate everything O thou, beloved of my twenty-seven senses, I love thine!

love and hate everything <u>*something or other.*</u>

love and hate everything *Frühe* **It was not only because they could serve as well as painter's pigment that Schwitters made use of the residues of life, the wretchedest of all materials.**

love and hate everything Cesar Domela *The king asked for a drink.*

love and hate everything The *Merzbau was a fabricated monument to the permanence and durability of his private, invented world, a* **luminous image,** *a point of order: stasis, a phantasmagoria, a dream grotto.*

love and hate everything logic and grammar People such as Huelsenbeck Moholy-Nagy *Blue singed flame murder very very down.*

love and hate everything *his private, invented world* an artist's loft Stein Piet Zwart *Sinking twists flat together spread askew.*

love and hate everything a luminous image trouble Satie Max Buchartz *Hollow burns the stomach flame sulfur blood.*

love and hate everything *a point of order: stasis* **the end of all** Klee Jan Tschichold *Remain true to duty, be faithful.*

love and hate everything *a phantasmagoria contradictoriness* Schoenberg Willi Baumeister *Those who change trains ravel knives slash bowels tremble.*

love and hate everything *a dream grotto* **A MARVELOUS DILETTANTE** respect, like, enjoy, or be delighted He designed posters, newspaper logos, theater schedules, and school cards for the cities of Hannover and Karlsruhe.

love and hate everything *Only three lusters has the creature bred in the glasshouse blossomed.*

love and hate everything *He had no choice but to play the clown.*

love and hate everything *THE MOST INTERNATIONAL* petit bourgeois *IN THE WORLD.*

love and hate everything *Merzbau Hannover,* begun by Schwitters around 1923 and continually worked upon for nearly fourteen years, was twenty years later--five years before his death--destroyed by Allied bombs.

love and hate everything posters Moon calf shines inward softly drew bowel fat pain softly drew bowel fat pain softly un-deafened.

love and hate everything (All for the Red Army.)

love and hate everything *not extending art into everyday life but subordinating external reality to one of his own making Go out into the whole world and make the truth known, the only truth there is, the truth about Anna Blume.*

love and hate everything <u>Now it is a Merzpicture.</u>

love and hate everything <u>Sorry!</u>

love and hate everything newspaper logos *Rotates servant girl twirling together draw and quarter railway engines twirl Emma Anna.*

love and hate everything *Threatening or disturbing images are themselves distorted through linguisitc inventiveness.*

love and hate everything <u>violet.</u>

love and hate everything *Merz ist form.*

love and hate everything theater schedules *Two mushrooms grew eyes stipe smooth bulbs milk and bored two holes in the king's belly.*

love and hate everything *Schlank stachelt Fisch in der Peitscheluft* scorned or scoffed at **loosening its ties to art** school cards **Words, sentences, parts of sentences, are cut out of some context and incorporated into a new context.**

love and hate everything Sleekly stabs fish in the whipair *ENTIRELY WITHOUT BOURGEOIS COMFORTS* Never believed he was making anything but pure abstract forms.

love and hate everything Schwitters continued to work as an artist through the last desperate decade of his life.

love and hate everything Schwitters believed the deadest language, the most outmoded ideas, can generate *Weltgefühl* **when they appear suddenly, unexpectedly, in an entirely unfamiliar setting.**

love and hate everything The Merzbarn evoked the wonder of a natural curiosity.

love and hate everything *His* **lifework** *was never finished.*

13 July 1988
New York

25th Merzgedicht in Memoriam *Kurt Schwitters*

erformerlecturertypographe *lter Bli* **raphic**

designer.paintersculptorwr *s a resul lter Bli* rgraphic

designermodern German art<u>Iraq Dates.Für Bieling</u>.**disaff rawn**

and written moti esclichésabsurd verbal

juxtapositionselements printed omething new from the

piecespenciled i believed itself an instrument of social r

ness an *d.Schlingen Arme breit* c advertising slogans**a frenzy**

of rhythmically reeling sentences, sentence fragments,

words, and word fragmentsabrupt reversions to logic*The*

princess winked and ordered that I be reassembled.Thus f c

advertising slogans**a frenzy of rhythmically reeling**

sentences, sentence fragments, words, and word

fragmentsabrupt reversions to logic*The princess winked and*

ordered that I be reassembled.Thus f c advertising slogans**a**

frenzy of rhythmically reeling sentences, sentence

fragments, words, and word fragmentsabrupt reversions to

logic*The princess winked and ordered that I be*

reassembled.Thus f eform.<u>Hansa.Fossil</u>.war and exileinterned

as an enemy alienan enemy alienspontaneous

encountersplayfully embraced every form or on top of the

rejected material.used tram tickets and stampsodd bits of

stationerywoodwire fabricspasted scraps o *injurious to art.*

THE MOST INTERNATIONAL petit bourge s--their meaning, their

sound, their appearance--had a central place in all of

Schwitters' endeavors, as a painter, sculptor, writer,

publisher, performer, lecturer, typographer, and g Berlin C

decoding. Word scraps, egenerate ArtSchwitters bega

Leninism. Hülsen ansformed into a work of art by a judicious

arrangement of forms around sive pos *terDie Märchen vom*

ParadiesMerz 21. e romantic l, newspaper logos, theater

schedules, and school cards for the cities of Hannover and

Karlsruhe. postersne *es Merz X ProgrammGefesse* m, Bussu **I**

whirl-heap Wilted wind's leaf Houses eyes men cliffs Bevel

whirl wind M *avy very very very very. Blau* m. Der

Sturm. Nächtlichhes D th cunning ingenuity and combined them

with intent to teaseIn *Arbeiterbild* red headlinelike letters

produce the effect of a revolutionary signal, an incitement

to rebellion. **Now and then a number, word, or phrase is**

written into s. *Merzzmalerei* **ma Social Security No. 097-4** *a*

work of art seems to me nted, a *hr a* th cunning ingenuity

and combined them with intent to teaseIn *Arbeiterbild* red

headlinelike letters produce the effect of a revolutionary

signal, an incitement to rebellion. **Now and then a number,**

word, or phrase is written into *delightful way* **ound child's**

head with the syph is consumer objec it was finally *rather*

sill sive pos love made up of word games, clichés, and

absurd ve **ound child's head with the syph** d Dada's

provocative individualism, and their tsnecessary to build

something new from the fragm **ig twisted-ar** d *my fightin*

erformerlecturertypographe *rienced th* vist ideas of

designVilmar Huszar*Kleine Dada SoiréeDie Scheuche*Ludwig

HilbersheimerKate Steinitza world of violent letter formsa

bottle of urine ascribed to GoetheIn the fourteen years

Schwitters worked on the *Merzbau* in Hannov *hitecture toda*

nterspasted scraps of papers with a b of

communicationVordembege-GildewartCesar DomelaMoholy-NagyPiet

ZwartMax BuchartzJan TschicholdWilli BaumeisterHe designed

posters *ten Lage Waffen verpflichtete alles.Anna received*

today in Weimar the following from.Before, the National

Assembly patchwork.As the first formation of a serious

situation weapons obliged everything.The many legible passag

sitc inventiveness.Schlank stachelt Fisch in der

*Peitscheluft*Sleekly stabs fish in the whipair**The Merb** f

papersmall wheelscandy wrappers **corridor with scattered**

camel *e instinctive and the* **pular.**Ursonate**a phonetic sound**

poem of considerable length with notations of his own de

ents, he or on top of the rejected material.used tram

tickets and stampsodd bits of stationerywoodwire

fabricspasted scraps o **to** *Merz.Hülsendadaismus = Husk*

DadaismI was a Dadaist without intending to be one.Ich wer

erformerlecturertypographe ion has been evoked.disparaged

the cult of provocative individualismsettled in Lysaker,

ansformed into a work of art by a judicious arrangement of

forms around *ves.All of us are born t* mages combined with

ordinary rubber-stamped messages used on packages to

indicate contents, mailing restrictions, or the name and

address of the senderThe revolutionary upheaval t *ention to*

the fact that people change a room b fftilfftoo?D **t and**

incorporated into a new context.Schwitters believed the

deadest language, the most outmoded ideas, can generate
Weltgefühl **when they appear suddenly, unexpectedly, i**
ansformed into a work of art by a judicious arrangement of
forms around umbers, meaningless in themselves, suggest the
real.never culled texts wi *by the motions* labelsglass spli
tible to the eye and of all required implements.It is
unimportant whether or not the material used in a *Merzbild*
was already formed for some purpose or other. A *Anna, weisst*
ied on wit g heute in Weimar folgendes aus.Von der
Nationalversammlung Stückwer rstes Veilchenheft.*"Die*
*Zoologischer Garten-*Lotterie*""Schacko"**Blood rinsed bucket**
blue ray red thick whip.The king asked for a drink.Blue
singed flame murder very very down.Sinking twists flat
together spread askew.Hollow burn utility**an extraordinary**
time*After the revolution I felt myself free and had t* hat
followed the armistice provided the break with the culture
of the past that was crucial **ding a huge k.***Als erste Bildung*
einer erns utility**an extraordinary time***After the revolution*
I felt myself free and had t erials Schwitters resu *holes*
in t pecially constructed for the purpose as well as
Merz-pictures that will restore by mechanical means the
balance dis e von prang from the same source ar Ambleside,
in the Lake Distric *en Röcke wogen Hals s Merz-pictures s h*
white mice ten Lage Waffen verpflichtete alles.Anna received
today in Weimar the following from.Before, the National
Assembly patchwork.As the first formation of a serious
situation weapons obliged everything.The many legible passag

showed *a ls tremble.Only three lusters has the crea* joined

a Dada groupStempelzeichnungen.s **tences, parts**

erformerlecturertypographe **n an entirely unfamilier**

setting.everyday-language banalitiesclichés of any kindpo th

cunning ingenuity and combined them with intent to teaseIn

Arbeiterbild red headlinelike letters produce the effect of

a revolutionary signal, an incitement to rebellion.**Now and**

then a number, word, or phrase is written into yllable taken

from a bank 10013-2441 212/2 n the *MERZbau* in **eJack**

14 July 1988
New York

26th Merzgedicht in Memoriam Kurt Schwitters

or disturbing images are themselves distorted through
Lysaker,
Kate Steinitz
ennze ziiuu rinnzkrrmüü; rakete bee bee.

De Stijl
Netzzeichnung.

used tram tickets and stamps
glass splinters
Hannah Höch
Marinetti
Piet Zwart
Suddenly the glorious revolution arrived!

up of word games, clichés, and
El Lissitzky
I felt myself free and had to cry
without commitments, he meant, *You*
Fossil.

necessary to build something new from the fragments
Weisst du es, Anna, weisst du es schon?

used tram tickets and stamps
wire
a ncw philosophy of social utility
Moholy-Nagy
Max Buchartz
a declaration of love
Vordemberge-Gildewart
Das Schwein niesst zum Herzen.

scraps of newsprint
Tatlin
wood
Tatlin
word or phrase is written into the picture freehand.

Schwitters escaped with his son to England
life in a long corridor with scattered camel dung
bureaucratic regulations
Walter Gropius
spontaneous encounters
whirl-heap Wilted wind's leaf Houses eyes men cliffs Bevel
Blau sengte Flamme Mord sehr ab sehr ab.

Apollinaire
the outbreak of hostilities
everyday life could be perceived as independent aesthetic.

glass splinters
scraps of newsprint
Pumpfftilff00?

wire
Heiss fischen Messer schiessen Blut.

Hülsendadaismus **is politically oriented, against art**
fabrics
pasted scraps of paper
newspaper logos
the last desperate decade of his life
Since only fools are modest,
Pumpfftilff00?

glass splinters
Merz: a syllable taken from a bank's letterhead, "*Kommer*z
interned as an enemy alien
returned to more open compositions.

After the revolution I felt myself free and had to cry out.

Netzzeichnung.

abandoned materials
I am went
Apollinaire
Der Sturm.

constructivist restraints
felt myself free and had.

Tatlin
Cubism
to cry out my jubilation to the world.

Suddenly the glorious revolution arrived!

His **lifework** *was never finished.*

dusted, washed, steamed, and dried.

wire netting
modern German art
Der Schlächter springt vor (Das ist die Liebe), schwingt.

Dada is making.

Degenerate Art
Whirl-heap blood's leaf
painter
active in other areas
kisses broad skirts surge white lacework kiss.

wire netting
pasted scraps of paper
Numbers, meaningless in themselves, suggest the real.

necessary to build something new from the pieces.

Big Love Grotto
modernism believed itself an instrument of social reform.

spontaneous encounters
His **lifework** *was never finished.*

Hülsenbeck wrote: *Dada is making propaganda.*

glass splinters
His **lifework** *was never finished.*

His **lifework** *was never finished.*

fantastic and mundane, in the *Merzbilder* begun in 1919.

Houses eyes men cliffs
together draw and quarter railway engines twirl.

small wheels
felt myself free and had to cry.

allusive possibilities
K Merzbild K4 (Bild rot Herz-Kirche).

a declaration of love
not far from Oslo, and began a second *Merzbau.*

I am went
glass splinters
Piet Zwart
confiscated from German museums in 1937 as Degenerate Art.

collages
candy wrappers
sharpen warm pipes smoothe slender legs
His **lifework** *was never finished.*

15 July 1988
New York

27th Merzgedicht in Memoriam Kurt Schwitters

Confiscated <u>Merzbild</u> El Lissitzky *wird gestraft!*

"*Lautsonate*" wood <u>Hansa</u>.

<u>Hansa</u>.

School cards Berlin *free* love ***sharpen*** **display** *significant,* page ***singed Speechless*** pasted ***Flamme Dadaist*** *felt* small wheels provocative Schwitters worked Max Buchartz desperate <u>Herzen</u>.

<u>**Nächtliches**</u> "*Lautsonate*" ***Merzmalerei*** **Hannah Höch** school cards abandoned materials shrink *grounds* **Ich** *Braunschweigenmotgeld* sculptor Max Buchartz *Architecture* **Hannah Höch** *Lamppost* word games *Gefesselter Blick* <u>Fossil</u>.

<u>Der Sturm</u>.

<u>Netzzeichnung</u>**.**

Allusive possibilities *Merzbau* used ***reassembled***.

Vordemberge-Gildewart *convinced* Vilmar Huszar Ludwig Hilbersheimer <u>K</u> Cubism <u>Das</u> De Stijl artist active **Ich taumeltürme Schwitters' application to join Club Dada was rejected.**

Finished.

Constructivist *Braunschweigenmotgeld **ziiuu*** **Menschen Norway** *All* wood **framework** *myself* Kate Steinitz outbreak *Everything destroyed* **Experiments** *mice.*

Wood *Braunschweigenmotgeld* **sulfur blood.**

Bussum, Bussum, Bussum.

Fragments "*Lautsonate*" Picabia **never finished.**

Obliged everything.

His **lifework** Constructive Composition.

El Lissitzky *His finished.*

Odd bits *Als Waffen* "*Lautsonate*" *Allgemeines Merz* **lifework** *never* restraints returned *cry out world.*

A luminous Image penciled on packages *Everything was necessary* ***smoothe neck pipes*** cotton wool Picabia *Merz erstes Veilchenheft.*

De Stijl *point order: stasis Everything necessary to build pieces.*

I most delightful with complete impartiality.

Clichés of kind wood **aggressive hostile Schwitters** Hans Arp drawings school cards and written motifs, pasted scraps constructivist restraints ***Merz-pictures inhabit constructed mechanical mice*** bureaucratic regulations interned as an enemy alien everyday-language banalities *finished His* **lifework** *His* **lifework** *was.*

24 July 1988
New York

28th *Merzgedicht* in Memoriam *Kurt Schwitters*

ennze ziiuu rinnzkrrmüü; rakete bee bee.

wood *and had to cry out my jubilation to the world.*

When the Germans invaded Norway in 1940, Schwitters escaped with his son to England, where they were interned for the first seventeen months.

wood Dada <u>Bussum, Bussum, Bussum.</u>

necessary to build something new from the fragments <u>Constructive Composition</u>.

"*Lautsonate*".

Als erste Bildung einer Lage Waffen verpflichtete alles.

penciled images combined with ordinary rubber-stamped messages used on packages to indicate contents, mailing restrictions, or the name and address of the sender <u>*Merz 21. erstes Veilchenheft*</u>.

De Stijl wood Hans Arp clichés of any kind *delightful way and as a result, I could introduce Dadaism into Holland with complete impartiality.*

Schwitters A r t i s a u t o n o m o u s.

difficult to reconcile *mir ist alles schnuppe, wenn ich meine schnauze auf die deine bautze position was anti-functionalist,* purely *artistic: a utopian* Satie **Schwitters' jovial and clownish nature** Satie Why make artworks if you're opposed to art?

lawfully allowed time **Du!**

Merz ist form.

Schwitters' expressive power was given direction by the scraps with which he created forms.

Tyll Eulenspiegel Schwitters' method is that from real avant-garde Klee **täglichen aufgebaut Bluemner oder** over possibilities available to artists.

Merz ist form.

Komposition infinity paradise paradise avant-garde chagrined *artistic unity* <u>**AVOID:**</u>
<u>**BECOMING THE CLASSICS OF TOMORROW.**</u>

Dadaists *Merzbild* **close friends found it difficult** Schwitters *Merzbild Merz ist form.*

Blau ist die Farbe Deines gelben Haares.

Chanson des autres is trouble **Du!**

avant-garde *Schwitters' method is that of Realism made from real things.*

A MARVELOUS DILETTANTE love and hate everything avant-garde *In* MERZ *his position was anti-functionalist, a conception.*

Entartete Kunst rubber-stamped messages ***Blood*** Vordemberge-Gildewart suggest the real.

Vordemberge-Gildewart *Entartete Kunst* **Now and then a number, word, or picture freehand.**

Max Buchartz theater schedules **abrupt reversions to logic** drawings *Ziiuu ennze ziiuu nnz krr müü, ziiuu ennze ziiuu rakete bee zee.*

used tram tickets and stamps *grew eyes stipe smooth belly.*

paper with a background stationery, torn photographs, wood, wire, fabric, small wheels, candy wrappers, labels, glass splinters, penciled images combined with ordinary rubber-stamped indicate contents, mailing restrictions, or the name and address Stempelzeichnungen.

Jackson Mac Low
27 - 28 August 1988
New York

29th Merzgedicht in Memoriam *Kurt Schwitters*

allen,
du bist labelsglass spli ar Ambleside,
in the Lake Distric **decade of his lifeThe slogans cut out** c advertising slogans**a frenzy of rhythmically reeling sentences,**
sentence fragments,
words,
and word fragmentsabrupt reversions to logic*The princess winked and ordered that I be reassembled.*

Thus f Zurich in entsgeometric simplicityA mis- or overprinted page of type was tr *en wie von d.*

Schlingen Arme breit f papersmall wheelscandy wrappers rbal juxtapositionsa declaration of loveword gam *e instinctive and the* **tone houses cliffsWhirl-heap blood** *eading.*

Meaningless elements stand alongside "clues,"
and no importance is attached to Berlin C **the picture freehand.**

I wonder whether we might not construct a system of weights to bring a person revolut
Waldhaus rgraphic designermodern German art<u>Iraq Dates</u>.

<u>Für Bieling</u>.

disaff rgraphic designermodern German art<u>Iraq Dates</u>.

<u>Für Bieling</u>.

disaff *nto Holland* **with t** astic and enstrasse in Ha <u>m,</u>
<u>Bussu</u> *es Merz X ProgrammGefesse* entsgeometric simplicityA mis- or overprinted page of type was tr **applied all the** *s servant girl twirling together draw and quarter railway engines twirl Emma Anna.*

Two mushrooms grew eyes stipe smooth bulbs milk a **wind's leaf**Ho *prang from the same source al presence of objects* **rouvés a picture of its creation**chagrine or on top of the rejected material.

used tram tickets and stampsodd bits of stationerywoodwire fabricspasted scraps o rbal juxtapositionsa declaration of loveword gam ion has been evoked.

disparaged the cult of provocative individualismsettled in Lysaker,
of communicationVordembege-GildewartCesar DomelaMoholy-NagyPiet ZwartMax
BuchartzJan TschicholdWilli BaumeisterHe designed posters mages combined with
ordinary rubber-stamped messages used on packages to indicate contents,
mailing restrictions,
or the name and address of the senderThe revolutionary upheaval t *uu,*
Uu see tee wee bee fümmmmms!

ned visual and verbal,
fant <u>orf</u>.

El LissitzkySchwitters' friends El Lissitzky ion has been evoked.

disparaged the cult of provocative individualismsettled in Lysaker,
Army.)

Rotate Army.)

Rotate parts *ly.*

**Words,
sen of sentences,
are of some contex n an entirely unfamiliar setting.**

everyday-language *banalitiesclichés* of any kindpo *med,
and dri d.*

*Schlingen Arme breit pitzen warme Röheen glatten schlank Füsse Karpfen,
Karpfen,
innzekete bee bee nnz krr g heute in Weimar folgendes aus.*

Von der Nationalversammlung Stückwer unhin ged.

Anna empfin k.

*Als erste Bildung einer erns free and had posterlik e,
thro wn into relief,
are absorbed* raps of newsprinttheater stubsstreetcar ticketsN *absolut e balance wit b a room
automatically.*

*Arc ention to the fact that people change a room b h white mice which inhabit pecially
constructed for the purpose as well as Merz-pictures that will restore by mechanical means the
balance dis delightful way* l association Norway in 1940,
**Schwitters escaped with his son to England,
where he was interned for of**
communicationVordembege-GildewartCesarDomelaMoholy-NagyPiet ZwartMax
BuchartzJan TschicholdWilli BaumeisterHe designed posters **he femal ig twisted-ar**

thought "An Anna Blume" d that *b sehr* it was finally *rather sill,*
even t hough a work of art seems to me m.

reduce romantic l ove to a bourgeo t*He dislike d my fightin g ways,*
said Hülsenbeck of Schwitters,
and I liked his static,
smug m **to Merz.**

Hülsendadaismus = Husk DadaismI was a Dadaist without intending to be one.

Ich wer 's leaf I am went **en stone houses cliffs Whirl-heap blood's leaf**To the Berlin Dada
group the Sturm group symbolized what was bankrupt in G *I am a painter and I nail my*
pictures together.

Art to Schwitters was as import ication to join Club Dada was rejected.

d durability of his private,
invented world,
a **luminous im arn evoked the wonder of a natural curiosity.**

His **lifework** *was never finished.*

29 August 1988
New York

30th Merzgedicht in Memoriam Kurt Schwitters

r schwer sehr sehr sehr sehr.

is love),
swings club,
*to lower lower heavy heavy fervently whips to e Grotte der Liebe*Big Love Grottot *turbed*
turbed vising to indicate rhythm,
timing,
and em Leninism.

Hülsen *sengte Flamme Mord se* indicate contents,
mailing and address of the senderThe revolutionary upheaval t litical catchwordsburea
splinters,
etc.

Constructive Compo wrappers,
labels,
glass splinters,
etc.

Constructive Compo e lava *e Revolutio* Arp"*An Anna Blume*"Hülsenbeck excluded
Schwitters from the **pular.**

*Ursonate*a phonetic sound poem of considerable length with notations of his own de
raphic designer.

paintersculptorwr *nto Holland e gegangen* Ich taumeltürme Welkes windes Blatt Häuser
Wind Menschen steinen Häuser Klippen Taumeltürme blutes Blatt.

*I am went*I whirl-heapWilted *y.*

(Herz-Kirche.)

29 - 30 August 1988
New York

31st Merzgedicht in Memoriam *Kurt Schwitters*

and for Charles O. Hartman

th the material.used petit performer,
Merz delightful tsnecessary twisted-ar designVilmar
Zoologischer
Merzgedicht
Merzgedicht in and moti verbal
Arme encountersplayfully material.used injurious international

Leninism.H
Karlsruhe.postersne
Bussu very letters signal,
ScheucheLudwig
Schwitters
Schwitters meaningless weisst timeAfter timeAfter
Schwitters banalitiesclich
Jackson
Mac
Jackson winked reassembled.Thus stationerywoodwire decoding.Word

M
ParadiesMerz incitement letters to
Now phrase way fightin eDie letter with many legible der
Merz.H change
Weltgef folgendes revolution
Merzgedicht
Merzgedicht fabricspasted injurious international meaning,
    central vom logos,
ProgrammGefesse teaseIn
Merzzmalerei arrangement king murder very flat spread
Schwitters
Schwitters
Schwitters raphic advertising encountersplayfully stationerywoodwire

Schwitters'
chtlichhes effect or effect revolutionary absurd erformerlecturertypographe
    ascribed hitecture
TschicholdWilli whipairThe erformerlecturertypographe

Veilchenheft."Die erformerlecturertypographe erformerlecturertypographe
    juxtapositionselements erformerlecturertypographe
    erformerlecturertypographe erformerlecturertypographe

erformerlecturertypographe erformerlecturertypographe
erformerlecturertypographe erformerlecturertypographe
erformerlecturertypographe erformerlecturertypographe
erformerlecturertypographe erformerlecturertypographe
letters lter lter eform.Hansa.Fossil.war bits place
painter,
rchen
ParadiesMerz syph rather ascribed
TschicholdWilli designed ten
Assembly serious obliged
Schlank considerable erformerlecturertypographe provocative
mages mailing change twists source paintersculptorwr
juxtapositionselements appearance--had
ScheucheLudwig
DomelaMoholy-NagyPiet rubber-stamped paintersculptorwr
alienspontaneous paintersculptorwr paintersculptorwr
stationerywoodwire scraps art.

rchen newspaper postersne
Blau headlinelike letters nted,
them
Soir bottle alles.Anna
Weimar rejected rgraphic
German disaff stampsodd
ArtSchwitters romantic communicationVordembege-GildewartCesar

DomelaMoholy-NagyPiet designed posters
National obliged
Schlank considerable erformerlecturertypographe groupStempelzeichnungen.s
designermodern reassembled.Thus exileinterned

HilbersheimerKate
DomelaMoholy-NagyPiet generate
Weltgef work forms already folgendes aus.Von drink.Blue extraordinary
armistice einer
MERZbau artIraq
Dates.F rawn moti itself words,
fragmentsabrupt reversions be winked frenzy reeling
Fossil.war encountersplayfully meaning,
decoding.Word sive pos
ParadiesMerz cliffs fftilfftoo?D real.never labelsglass
ckwer drink.Blue askew.Hollow and had with crucial
utilityan felt constructed source teaseIn
MERZbau
Low 25th designer.paintersculptorwr esclich as encountersplayfully
sculptor,
publisher,
chtlichhes

ScheucheLudwig
Steinitza
Hannov fabricspasted messages language,
appear folgendes
Von der
Garten-Lotterie""Schacko"Blood combined signal,
rebellion.Now
Jackson
July juxtapositionselements omething social nterspasted
    patchwork.As wrappers instinctive incorporated
    juxtapositionselements stationerywoodwire
communicationVordembege-GildewartCesar
    individualismsettled
Garten-Lotterie""Schacko"Blood juxtapositionselements

HilbersheimerKate juxtapositionselements individualismsettled
    groupStempelzeichnungen.s juxtapositionselements
    juxtapositionselements printed from princess frenzy
    petit bourge individualism,
of umbers,
themselves,
texts whether material teaseIn omething new believed newspaper
    for
ProgrammGefesse produce seems to th them produce signal,
then clich
HilbersheimerKate scraps piecespenciled instrument
Schlingen piecespenciled individualism,
groupStempelzeichnungen.s piecespenciled stationerywoodwire
    injurious bourge meaning,
all
Leninism.H cities
Hannover combined combined intent it was sive bottle fftilfftoo?D
    and incorporated into unexpectedly,
ansformed texts material revolution incitement
Schwitters piecespenciled instrument of of sentences,
words,
encountersplayfully petit appearance--had school red
Now
Merzzmalerei was twisted-ar ascribed on
DomelaMoholy-NagyPiet serious
Schlank
Ich mailing
Schwitters suddenly,
meaningless folgendes utilityan and armistice timeAfter
    myself by prang the
National first crea a advertising reversions ordered advertising
    logicThe advertising princess international arrangement
    advertising slogansa slogansa slogansa fragments,

Hansa.Fossil.war encountersplayfully tickets
papersmall fabricspasted erformerlecturertypographe
been born frenzy frenzy of of rhythmically that avy
letters clich erformerlecturertypographe
GoetheIn communicationVordembege-GildewartCesar
Ursonatea individualismsettled unexpectedly,
rhythmically reeling sentences,
frenzy reeling reeling sentences,
meaning,
sound,
central
Leninism.H postersne
Wilted cunning wheelscandy scattered notations stampsodd

Merz.H ion cult rubber-stamped contents,
restrictions,
Schwitters forms around meaningless suggest
Assembly obliged teaseIn fragments,
fragmentsabrupt winked words,
word words,
reassembled.Thus and an and writer,
Word scraps,
terDie for
ProgrammGefesse leaf fragm
Assembly obliged stationerywoodwire provocative judicious
        rubber-stamped fragmentsabrupt fragmentsabrupt
        fragmentsabrupt fragmentsabrupt fragmentsabrupt
        reversions be advertising reversions ordered alienspontaneous
        s--their rebellion.Now incitement
Schwitters the toda
Lage today legible individualismsettled judicious
Schwitters everything.The groupStempelzeichnungen.s parts
        erformerlecturertypographe written paintersculptorwr
        logicThc princess slogansa princess winked winked

Hansa.Fossil.war tickets place around and and and of or and
        intent absurd tsnecessary twisted-ar th the years
        posters in
Before,
serious rejected
Merz.H that weisst rstes source incitement reassembled.Thus
        reassembled.Thus reassembled.Thus
ScheucheLudwig to the fourteen first formation corridor and
        address revolutionary upheaval incorporated
Schwitters
Zoologischer paintersculptorwr juxtapositionselements
        advertising advertising slogansa slogansa eform.Hansa.Fossil.war

ProgrammGefesse signal,
cunning letters papersmall fabricspasted erformerlecturertypographe
      been born frenzy frenzy of of rhythmically that avy
      letters clich erformerlecturertypographe
GoetheIn communicationVordembege-GildewartCesar
Ursonatea individualismsettled unexpectedly,
rhythmically reeling sentences,
frenzy reeling reeling sentences,
meaning,
sound,
central
Leninism.H postersne
Wilted cunning wheelscandy scattered notations stampsodd

Merz.H ion cult rubber-stamped contents,
restrictions,
Schwitters forms around meaningless suggest
Assembly obliged teaseIn fragments,
fragmentsabrupt winked words,
word words,
reassembled.Thus and an and writer,
Word scraps,
terDie for
ProgrammGefesse leaf fragm
Assembly obliged stationerywoodwire provocative judicious
      rubber-stamped fragmentsabrupt fragmentsabrupt
      fragmentsabrupt fragmentsabrupt fragmentsabrupt
      reversions be advertising reversions ordered alienspontaneous
      s--their rebellion.Now incitement
Schwitters the toda
Lage today legible individualismsettled judicious
Schwitters everything.The groupStempelzeichnungen.s parts
      erformerlecturertypographe written paintersculptorwr
      logicThe princess slogansa princess winked winked

Hansa.Fossil.war tickets place around and and and of or and
      intent absurd tsnecessary twisted-ar th the years
      posters in
Before,
serious rejected
Merz.H that weisst rstes source incitement reassembled.Thus
      reassembled.Thus reassembled.Thus
ScheucheLudwig to the fourteen first formation corridor and
      address revolutionary upheaval incorporated
Schwitters
Zoologischer paintersculptorwr juxtapositionselements
      advertising advertising slogansa slogansa eform.Hansa.Fossil.war

ProgrammGefesse signal,
cunning letters papersmall fabricspasted erformerlecturertypographe
        been born frenzy frenzy of of rhythmically that avy
        letters clich erformerlecturertypographe
GoetheIn communicationVordembege-GildewartCesar
Ursonatea individualismsettled unexpectedly,
rhythmically reeling sentences,
frenzy reeling reeling sentences,
meaning,
sound,
central
Leninism.H postersne
Wilted cunning wheelscandy scattered notations stampsodd

Merz.H ion cult rubber-stamped contents,
restrictions,
Schwitters forms around meaningless suggest
Assembly obliged teaseIn fragments,
fragmentsabrupt winked words,
word words,
reassembled.Thus and an and writer,
Word scraps,
terDie for
ProgrammGefesse leaf fragm
Assembly obliged stationerywoodwire provocative judicious
        rubber-stamped fragmentsabrupt fragmentsabrupt
        fragmentsabrupt fragmentsabrupt fragmentsabrupt
        reversions be advertising reversions ordered alienspontaneous
        s--their rebellion.Now incitement
Schwitters the toda
Lage today legible individualismsettled judicious
Schwitters everything.The groupStempelzeichnungen.s parts
        erformerlecturertypographe written paintersculptorwr
        logicThe princess slogansa princess winked winked

Hansa.Fossil.war tickets place around and and and of or and
        intent absurd tsnecessary twisted-ar th the years
        posters in
Before,
serious rejected
Merz.H that weisst rstes source incitement reassembled.Thus
        reassembled.Thus reassembled.Thus
ScheucheLudwig to the fourteen first formation everything.The
        of evoked.disparaged address
Assembly has
Dada tences,
teaseIn signal,

from
Low designer.paintersculptorwr sabsurd
Schlingen
Fossil.war war material.used scraps art.

international endeavors,
egenerate extraordinary utilityan well
Ambleside,
Distric teaseIn fragments,
exileinterned
Merzzmalerei
HuszarKleine
HilbersheimerKate fabricspasted a us are on ention and the
    outmoded today
Assembly yllable
Bli
Dates.F alienan central decoding.Word egenerate ansformed
    theater them today
Assembly
All mailing name arrangement umbers,
piecespenciled reversions reversions alienspontaneous
    revolutionary everyday-language piecespenciled
    alienspontaneous alienspontaneous alienspontaneous
    encountersplayfully on tickets typographer,
Bussu cunning revolutionary incitement
Schwitters fabricspasted encountersplayfully groupStempelzeichnungen.s
    encountersplayfully encountersplayfully encountersplayfully
    encountersplayfully encountersplayfully
PeitscheluftSleekly encountersplayfully embraced umbers,
    labelsglass extraordinary timeAfter balance received
    combined effect every the fabricspasted today following
    formation serious poem of or on and to to appear of of
    themselves,
the the required
Merzbild rejected material.used
ArtSchwitters romantic
Hannover combined
Merzzmalerei ma art ingenuity absurd individualism,
nterspasted
National
Ursonatea used lsendadaismus used to or that room t wi bucket

Sinking erste utilityan serious a
Only
Dada s lter fragments,
enemy stampsodd scraps injurious combined scattered bits
    without intending messages on of senderThe
It flame flat utilityan extraordinary teaseIn headlinelike

Schwitters stationerywoodwire
TschicholdWilli stationerywoodwire stationerywoodwire
    stationerywoodwire stationerywoodwire stationerywoodwire
    paintersculptorwr stationerywoodwire fabricspasted
    painter,
publisher,
whirl-heap chtlichhes produce letters fabricspasted individualismsettled

Schwitters arrangement
Garten-Lotterie""Schacko"Blood exileinterned stampsodd
    scraps performer,
scraps,
newspaper cities of
I ingenuity objec absurd their fightin patchwork.As individualismsettled
    judicious t combined and art motions tible the eye
    material formed aus.Von
Garten-Lotterie""Schacko"Blood
I and hat huge einer mechanical
National ingenuity juxtapositionselements international

HuszarKleine international
TschicholdWilli posters ten
National serious scattered bits to heute extraordinary prang
    source s white patchwork.As obliged ingenuity
Arbeiterbild
MERZbau
New fragments,
princess reeling sentences,
reeling to that enemy petit their sound,
Word
Houses cunning child's the child's the individualism,
their ascribed upheaval appear umbers,
already
Weimar
Nationalversammlung
Veilchenheft."Die
Zoologischer constructed appearance--had appearance--had
    appearance--had a central performer,
Leninism.H postersne
ProgrammGefesse formsa
Assembly patchwork.As
All that thick singed
I and armistice
Als
Bildung of of signal,
Schwitters
Schwitters

Schwitters'
publisher,
romantic revolutionary incitement
Schwitters fabricspasted erformerlecturertypographe individualismsettled
    judicious mages messages upheaval incorporated
    together sentences,
and as an petit painter,
writer,
egenerate theater incitement whipairThe scattered scraps
    heute
Veilchenheft."Die groupStempelzeichnungen.s intent juxtapositionselements
    s--their writer,
ArtSchwitters whirl-heap
Wilted
Houses letters produce number,
Arbeiterbild child's ascribed scraps
TschicholdWilli
PeitscheluftSleekly stationerywoodwire provocative ves.All
    born ansformed motions required incitement
Schwitters
Schwitters lter designer.paintersculptorwr esclich juxtapositionselements
    encountersplayfully appearance--had lecturer,
    Hannover th syph syph erformerlecturertypographe
    designVilmar
HuszarKleine nterspasted fabricspasted
Veilchenheft."Die constructed
Merz-pictures ar in today groupStempelzeichnungen.s banalitiesclich
    teaseIn word,
Bieling.disaff esclich
Schlingen c decoding.Word bega incitement into child's individualism,
    fightin disparaged work forms born used senderThe

Schwitters work arrangement unimportant purpose extraordinary
    rgraphic
Bieling.disaff rawn piecespenciled appearance--had typographer,
    egenerate arrangement around
ProgrammGefesse chtlichhes teaseIn effect delightful
ArtSchwitters revolutionary nterspasted communicationVordembege-GildewartCesar
    verpflichtete revolutionary
Merz-pictures by mechanical wogen
Anna legible tences,
banalitiesclich incitement taken
Memoriam slogansa
Leninism.H
H lsen es eyes cunning and intent was
Waffen following disparaged ansformed indicate ansformed
    into in motions
Blood asked with holes for bank omething of an

Arme material.used bits typographer,
and judicious
Bussu and incitement effect individualism,
patchwork.As individualismsettled judicious arrangement
    around born ideas,
arrangement
Zoologischer together
Memoriam exileinterned arrangement fabricspasted o of forms
    born work forms themselves,
and or
Zoologischer resu balance showed s kindpo revolutionary rebellion.Now
    phrase
Low designer.paintersculptorwr the believed words,
word reeling fragments,
material.used rchen schedules,
school
Bevel ingenuity ve to something papers
BaumeisterHe verpflichtete
Anna sound notations rejected rubber-stamped groupStempelzeichnungen.s
    erformerlecturertypographe typographer,
ParadiesMerz e romantic logos,
combined phrase ingenuity intent rebellion.Now
communicationVordembege-GildewartCesar

Lage
National serious new weisst groupStempelzeichnungen.s
MERZbau piecespenciled instrument encountersplayfully
    lecturer,
Word bega into forms terDie theater the phrase written incitement
    whipairThe scattered scraps
Ich mages
Blood revolution crucial timeAfter sentences,
and and ordered slogansa scraps
Schwitters'
typographer,
ansformed school cards
Hannover
Karlsruhe.postersne wind's phrase finally pos word the their
    the communicationVordembege-GildewartCesar first
    situation obliged phonetic stampsodd of of hl labelsglass

Anna,
drink.Blue
Hollow received legible erformerlecturertypographe an entirely
    and
Kurt
Jackson
Merzgedicht

Bieling.disaff words,
appearance--had
Karlsruhe.postersne chtlichhes
Merzzmalerei produce to was vist
HilbersheimerKate letter
BaumeisterHe following inventiveness.Schlank e used
Merz.H be wer
Merzbild
X
ProgrammGefesse
Arbeiterbild produce fragm erformerlecturertypographe
　　　formsa
DomelaMoholy-NagyPiet arrangement following erformerlecturertypographe

ProgrammGefesse headlinelike inventiveness.Schlank individualismsettled

Garten-Lotterie""Schacko"Blood murder burn culture past
　　　erns produce incitement word,
phrase written lter resul esclich piecespenciled rhythmically
　　　whirl-heap
Wilted wind's delightful vist
HilbersheimerKate worked with first many used stampsodd lsendadaismus
　　　be that ansformed heute folgendes blue twists erste
　　　erials e typographer,
egenerate
ArtSchwitters
M newspaper
Hannover cliffs
Blau written
Waffen verpflichtete papersmall bits
Merz.H revolutionary upheaval people
Weltgef when unimportant extraordinary revolution with ding
　　　einer kindpo
MERZbau a every avy very very very very.Blau ve head world many
　　　ves.All messages work very very revolution for many
　　　banalitiesclich yllable eJack resul moti d.Schlingen
　　　reeling words,
slogansa stampsodd bourge whirl-heap
Sturm.N
N chtlichhes th with child's ascribed
TschicholdWilli everything.The senderThe unexpectedly,
　　　meaningless der thick whip.The culture huge einer
　　　means received
National setting.everyday-language ingenuity and signal,
　　　rebellion.Now taken instrument advertising fragments,
　　　ingenuity and intent red cunning combined number,
　　　HilbersheimerKate ascribed communicationVordembege-GildewartCesar

designed received today the the formation weapons
sitc with with intending one.Ich into mages ordinary

Schwitters the most they meaningless real.never weisst heute

Distric teaseIn
Arbeiterbild produce rebellion.Now taken
Schwitters
Schwitters erformerlecturertypographe designer.paintersculptorwr

Arbeiterbild headlinelike
Arbeiterbild incorporated real.never never and heute
Weimar flame murder revolution
Distric teaseIn headlinelike erformerlecturertypographe

Arbeiterbild headlinelike headlinelike letters revolutionary
        into vist
HilbersheimerKate letter
BaumeisterHe posters from.Before,
phonetic used language,
balance received today the the everything.The of effect rebellion.Now
        logicThe advertising of of and reversions be sive
        logos,
whirl-heap ingenuity revolutionary revolutionary revolutionary
        arrangement extraordinary extraordinary revolutionary
        signal,
Bieling.disaff logicThe princess slogansa
Fossil.war and an injurious international lecturer,
Leninism.H theater incitement incitement
ScheucheLudwig formation incorporated the most real.never
        never labelsglass material revolution pecially

Merz-pictures formation situation n combined
Now and into and the rhythmically reeling princess and newspaper

Bussu combined number,
teaseIn letters word,
consumer word ound of urine papers the first pular.Ursonatea
        forms people incorporated is whether or weisst heute
        twists source teaseIn incitement and into
Memoriam
Schwitters
Mac
Merzgedicht
Kurt
Merz
Merzzmalerei consumer provocative
HuszarKleine

HilbersheimerKate
BaumeisterHe verpflichtete
Merzzmalerei ma way syph consumer ascribed designed
Weimar legible sitc der tickets around restrictions,
judicious suggest pecially
National formation a weapons joined parts bank omething of
    an
Arme material.used stampsodd petit their forms logos,
theater for
Merz leaf
N nted,
them headlinelike a head provocative and their the
communicationVordembege-GildewartCesar

BuchartzJan ten phonetic considerable combined mailing incorporated
    into suggest never balance serious situation ingenuity
    ingenuity and intent red cunning combined number,
    HilbersheimerKate ascribed communicationVordembege-GildewartCesar
    designed received today the the formation weapons
    sitc with with intending one.Ich into mages ordinary

Schwitters the most they meaningless real.never weisst heute

Distric teaseIn
Arbeiterbild produce rebellion.Now taken
Schwitters
Schwitters erformerlecturertypographe designer.paintersculptorwr

Arbeiterbild headlinelike
Arbeiterbild incorporated real.never never and heute
Weimar flame murder revolution
Distric teaseIn headlinelike erformerlecturertypographe

Arbeiterbild headlinelike headlinelike letters revolutionary
    into vist
HilbersheimerKate letter
BaumeisterHe posters from.Before,
phonetic used language,
balance received today the the everything.The of effect rebellion.Now
    logicThe advertising of of and reversions be sive
    logos,
whirl-heap ingenuity revolutionary revolutionary revolutionary
    arrangement extraordinary extraordinary revolutionary
    signal,
Bieling.disaff logicThe princess slogansa
Fossil.war and an injurious international lecturer,
Leninism.H theater incitement incitement
ScheucheLudwig formation incorporated the most real.never

never labelsglass material revolution pecially

Merz-pictures formation situation n combined
Now and into and the rhythmically reeling princess and newspaper

Bussu combined number,
teaseIn letters word,
consumer word ound of urine papers the first pular.Ursonatea
    forms people incorporated is whether or weisst heute
    twists source teaseIn incitement and into
Memoriam designer.paintersculptorwr resul believed social
    bourge
ArtSchwitters revolutionary delightful delightful individualism,
    world
Hannov ray of huge einer kindpo cunning them written
Bieling.disaff sound,
Leninism.H
H terDie leaf wind with signal,
into with to the then syph syph papers with in
Assembly corridor sound considerable ents,
language,
implements.It purpose together of obliged rejected material.used

ArtSchwitters into
Sturm.N with ma was finally sill ound
Dada's bottle verpflichtete already rstes
Garten-Lotterie""Schacko"Blood extraordinary with erste
    constructed same
Distric
Hals following serious situation revolutionary rebellion.Now
    phrase
Low designer.paintersculptorwr lter moti advertising reversions
    material.used fabricspasted endeavors,
sive up upheaval outmoded of wi motions
Merzbild murder groupStempelzeichnungen.s parts combined
    intent phrase c slogansa princess place clich s,
and individualism,
and ascribed obliged passag around restrictions,
outmoded
Von der of huge einer kindpo cunning them written
Bieling.disaff sound,
Leninism.H
H terDie leaf wind with signal,
into with to the then syph syph papers with
DomelaMoholy-NagyPiet designed
Lage today pular.Ursonatea stampsodd provocative art around
    provided purpose balance
National ingenuity juxtapositionselements provocative

verpflichtete in inventiveness.Schlank and individualismsettled
individualism,
fightin rienced individualismsettled incorporated mechanical
juxtapositionselements individualism,
individualismsettled ansformed into judicious t the the ention
incorporated the is
Anna,
ckwer
Veilchenheft."Die source serious paintersculptorwr rhythmically
exileinterned tsnecessary to something bottle
BuchartzJan
Weimar following sound stampsodd to combined name twists together
armistice following
ProgrammGefesse
N teaseIn
Now finally provocative from formsa to the the following from.Before,
weapons length
Assembly ingenuity rgraphic the twisted-ar
Soir first scattered
Lysaker,
folgendes mechanical unfamilier designer.paintersculptorwr
moti typographer,
forms sive logos,
with incitement
Security teaseIn effect or erformerlecturertypographe
Before,
papersmall erformerlecturertypographe arrangement incorporated
erformerlecturertypographe erformerlecturertypographe
erformerlecturertypographe verpflichtete erformerlecturertypographe
erformerlecturertypographe erformerlecturertypographe
erformerlecturertypographe erformerlecturertypographe
erformerlecturertypographe erformerlecturertypographe
erformerlecturertypographe erformerlecturertypographe
erformerlecturertypographe erformerlecturertypographe
erformerlecturertypographe erformerlecturertypographe
erformerlecturertypographe red signal,
then paintersculptorwr logicThe princess ordered that
Thus vom cities postersne
Wilted ingenuity ideas
Steinitza toda nterspasted of of
DomelaMoholy-NagyPiet designed posters
National obliged
Schlank designVilmar everything.The
PeitscheluftSleekly designVilmar revolutionary
Zoologischer
Hollow burn myself
Merz-pictures mechanical
Weimar

HuszarKleine
National inventiveness.Schlank
Arbeiterbild exileinterned fabricspasted decoding.Word

ParadiesMerz and phrase s.Merzzmalerei
Social written
Soir eDie address unimportant material some
Schacko"Blood
Schwitters holes produce raphic esclich piecespenciled reassembled.Thus

ScheucheLudwig nterspasted
ScheucheLudwig banalitiesclich
ScheucheLudwig
HilbersheimerKate violent alles.Anna stabs phonetic disparaged
    address senderThe unexpectedly,
Arbeiterbild
HilbersheimerKate
BaumeisterHe
Garten-Lotterie""Schacko"Blood
HilbersheimerKate
DomelaMoholy-NagyPiet individualismsettled everyday-language
    s lter lter designermodern alienan material.used

Schwitters'
Steinitza communicationVordembege-GildewartCesar
Waffen today first
Schlank sound of of ves.All with people real.never culled motions
    timeAfter
Lake
Merz-pictures
National lusters joined letters from
Low
York
German
Dates.F alienan bits to art.

most whirl-heap incitement or of up provocative build rienced

HilbersheimerKate ascribed
TschicholdWilli received everything.The corridor
Assembly legible combined them to
German moti omething instrument rhythmically fragments,
    reversions appearance--had typographer,
theater the finally pos fourteen years
ZwartMax
Before,
legible notations yllable
MERZbau eJack lter

Dates.F sabsurd
Schlingen
Schwitters'
Schwitters
TschicholdWilli formation
Ursonatea stationerywoodwire
Schwitters meaningless wi motions
Merzbild bucket singed spread of and t the the
Merz-pictures ten verpflichtete
MERZbau
Merzbau
DomelaMoholy-NagyPiet constructed in en
Hals
Lage
Anna joined performer,
Hannover
Houses wind chtlichhes ingenuity effect intent
Merzbau hitecture
BaumeisterHe ten today and pular.Ursonatea notations stampsodd
    lsendadaismus address ideas,
Merz-pictures
National paintersculptorwr
ArtSchwitters
ParadiesMerz
ScheucheLudwig
Steinitza
Schwitters worked toda scraps papers of of passag papersmall
    top rejected material.used stampsodd was without
    intending with and b outmoded of culled motions some

Weimar culture
Bildung
Merz-pictures mechanical rhythmically alienspontaneous
    individualism,
communicationVordembege-GildewartCesar juxtapositionselements
    communicationVordembege-GildewartCesar
communicationVordembege-GildewartCesar
    erformerlecturertypographe communicationVordembege-GildewartCesar
    stationerywoodwire communicationVordembege-GildewartCesar
    communicationVordembege-GildewartCesar
communicationVordembege-GildewartCesar
    communicationVordembege-GildewartCesar
communicationVordembege-GildewartCesar
    communicationVordembege-GildewartCesar
communicationVordembege-GildewartCesar
    communicationVordembege-GildewartCesar
communicationVordembege-GildewartCesar
    communicationVordembege-GildewartCesar

communicationVordembege-GildewartCesar
    communicationVordembege-GildewartCesar
communicationVordembege-GildewartCesar
    communicationVordembege-GildewartCesar
communicationVordembege-GildewartCesar
    communicationVordembege-GildewartCesar
communicationVordembege-GildewartCesar
    communicationVordembege-GildewartCesar
communicationVordembege-GildewartCesar

DomelaMoholy-NagyPiet posters camel rejected revolutionary
    language,
ansformed formation typographer,
DomelaMoholy-NagyPiet considerable unexpectedly,
designermodern
HilbersheimerKate
DomelaMoholy-NagyPiet
DomelaMoholy-NagyPiet
DomelaMoholy-NagyPiet
DomelaMoholy-NagyPiet
DomelaMoholy-NagyPiet juxtapositionselements
ZwartMax own tram fabricspasted twists erformerlecturertypographe
    everyday-language
ZwartMax
BuchartzJan pular.Ursonatea tickets without disparaged
    ansformed indicate
Steinitza
BuchartzJan rubber-stamped restrictions,
the is bucket with crucial balance everything.The rebellion.Now
    erformerlecturertypographe
TschicholdWilli stationerywoodwire
Merzzmalerei
TschicholdWilli
PeitscheluftSleekly groupStempelzeichnungen.s banalitiesclich
    taken
Thus enemy tickets injurious
Leninism.H ingenuity
Merzzmalerei tsnecessary
BaumeisterHe considerable de he
Husk individualismsettled change suddenly,
arrangement required purpose folgendes aus.Von
Garten-Lotterie""Schacko"Blood rinsed murder serious
The legible tences,
letters taken page
Dates.F written sabsurd effect
Waffen phonetic combined
Von der
Garten-Lotterie""Schacko"Blood whip.The verpflichtete

legible ingenuity rgraphic typographer,
ArtSchwitters
Merzzmalerei erformerlecturertypographe verpflichtete
    alles.Anna
All believed generate forms around in
Anna,
Schacko"Blood rinsed red pecially same received believed
    embraced rejected tram to endeavors,
scraps,
today in inventiveness.Schlank whipairThe
Merb mailing room appear ansformed themselves,
the the formed for folgendes
Veilchenheft."Die
Zoologischer
Hollow armistice following
ProgrammGefesse finally provocative from formsa bottle years

Waffen
Before,
papersmall wrappers the phonetic poem notations material.used
    bits individualismsettled ansformed combined upheaval
    meaningless and is was already
Assembly ascribed
Assembly ordinary packages mailing ention thick patchwork.As
    following patchwork.As corridor patchwork.As
As ls tremble.Only three the from
Bieling.disaff verbal ness breit frenzy words,
word enemy embraced rejected s--their rebellion.Now incitement
    or of and syph new world designed following serious
    weapons sitc
Fisch with around messages
Schwitters
Zoologischer formation situation weapons legible teaseIn
    verpflichtete following
National serious obliged obliged
Only entirely
Merzgedicht
Merzgedicht sabsurd eform.Hansa.Fossil.war every the fabricspasted
    today formation everything.The
DadaismI utilityan everything.The
The showed tremble.Only
MERZbau
Jackson sentences,
very letters revolutionary signal,
incitement
Merzbau verpflichtete received patchwork.As many passag
    considerable disparaged arrangement senderThe
    wi motions thick

I and revolution myself balance formation situation inventiveness.Schlank
    disparaged arrangement incorporated
Nationalversammlung
Merz-pictures same
Schwitters
Schwitters
Bieling.disaff verbal
Schlingen
HuszarKleine
Soir
Steinitza years patchwork.As stachelt wrappers suddenly,
    unexpectedly,
forms wi was thick patchwork.As ingenuity and designer.paintersculptorwr
    resul rgraphic printed new princess that reassembled.Thus
    embraced publisher,
performer,
headlinelike
ScheucheLudwig
PeitscheluftSleekly erformerlecturertypographe
Merz-pictures
TschicholdWilli
PeitscheluftSleekly
PeitscheluftSleekly
PeitscheluftSleekly individualismsettled encountersplayfully
    stampsodd stationerywoodwire meaning,
combined phrase finally sill pos with individualism,
and their the rienced world the
Weimar weapons passag whipairThe wrappers instinctive
Veilchenheft."Die constructed
Merz-pictures restore
Merz-pictures combined from page raphic top rejected material.used
    stampsodd performer,
papersmall erformerlecturertypographe individualismsettled
    work the the upheaval people deadest unexpectedly,
    utilityan utilityan
TschicholdWilli wheelscandy wrappers
Ursonatea tram disparaged unexpectedly,
themselves,
unimportant
Zoologischer culture holes for source received showed juxtapositionselements
    s--their writer,
sive cities with signal,
ScheucheLudwig years posters first obliged whipairThe scattered
    stampsodd cult mages combined name revolutionary
    ention incorporated into most
Weltgef meaningless motions
Distric ingenuity juxtapositionselements provocative verpflichtete
    alles.Anna

Anna today the the the passag pular.Ursonatea cult
Lysaker,
restrictions,
upheaval art was
Blood balance
MERZbau
Schwitters
Schwitters rhythmically princess that slogansa frenzy sentences,
    logicThe advertising rhythmically sentences,
words,
Thus meaning,
sound,
place
Word egenerate forms of effect cunning combined ound consumer
    ascribed worked designed patchwork.As
Ursonatea considerable unexpectedly,
Garten-Lotterie""Schacko"Blood
Lake
Merz-pictures ten slogansa petit
ArtSchwitters work sive cities with
Now word,
into phrase written individualism,
patchwork.As notations judicious of of hl wi was or twists ding
    dis
Merz-pictures everything.The
Only entirely teaseIn headlinelike letters of or omething
    an to logicThe top of of to
The their rchen newspaper objec sive tsnecessary
Schwitters designed received many passag sitc inventiveness.Schlank
    papersmall notations material.used upheaval unexpectedly,
    is whether used thick drink.Blue flame from the
Distric mice bank piecespenciled advertising slogansa and
    and ordered slogansa stampsodd stationerywoodwire
    forms newspaper cities patchwork.As rejected stampsodd
    bits without intending messages on of senderThe
It flame flat utilityan extraordinary teaseIn headlinelike

Schwitters stationerywoodwire
TschicholdWilli stationerywoodwire stationerywoodwire
    stationerywoodwire stationerywoodwire stationerywoodwire
    paintersculptorwr stationerywoodwire fabricspasted
    painter,
publisher,
whirl-heap chtlichhes produce letters fabricspasted individualismsettled

Schwitters arrangement
Garten-Lotterie""Schacko"Blood exileinterned stampsodd
    scraps performer,

scraps,
newspaper cities of th combined
Merzzmalerei
Security work
HuszarKleine
HilbersheimerKate letter ascribed
GoetheIn
Hannov sound lsendadaismus individualismsettled utilityan
extraordinary
Schwitters
HilbersheimerKate lsendadaismus
Merz-pictures
Hals lusters has bank designer.paintersculptorwr paintersculptorwr
and scraps meaning,
publisher,
performer,
ArtSchwitters work
ParadiesMerz postersne avy
Der ma and phrase ascribed scraps
BuchartzJan
Waffen first situation fish without revolutionary context.Schwitters
ideas,
unexpectedly,
into umbers,
balance showed ingenuity appearance--had
ProgrammGefesse th combined build new of on the in scraps
Schlank whipairThe
Merb corridor e
Ursonatea erformerlecturertypographe into restrictions,
implements.It purpose together erformerlecturertypographe
erformerlecturertypographe erformerlecturertypographe
verpflichtete erformerlecturertypographe erformerlecturertypographe
erformerlecturertypographe erformerlecturertypographe
erformerlecturertypographe erformerlecturertypographe
erformerlecturertypographe erformerlecturertypographe
erformerlecturertypographe erformerlecturertypographe
erformerlecturertypographe erformerlecturertypographe
erformerlecturertypographe erformerlecturertypographe
ingenuity combined bank
Hansa.Fossil.war war most bourge meaning,
their sound,
endeavors,
avy produce work teaseIn absurd d fightin vist verpflichtete

Weimar disparaged provocative omething exileinterned
TschicholdWilli ten the the corridor pular.Ursonatea cult
contents,
or of people art around provided purpose balance

National ingenuity juxtapositionselements provocative
verpflichtete in inventiveness.Schlank and individualismsettled
individualism,
fightin rienced individualismsettled incorporated mechanical
juxtapositionselements individualism,
individualismsettled juxtapositionselements
ProgrammGefesse
HilbersheimerKate erformerlecturertypographe individualismsettled
juxtapositionselements individualismsettled
in ansformed language,
by was
Anna,
thick source paintersculptorwr a and itself performer,
ansformed
Karlsruhe.postersne
ProgrammGefesse whirl-heap scattered instinctive and with
erformerlecturertypographe ansformed work forms
born packages or of a art motions
Blood myself and joined cunning and incitcmcnt logicThe exileinterned
stampsodd injurious endeavors,
as writer,
performer,
scraps,
Leninism.H arrangement
ParadiesMerz
ProgrammGefesse chtlichhes revolutionary fabricspasted
o of forms born work forms themselves,
and or
Zoologischer resu balance showed verbal new itself an slogansa
all of of up tsnecessary ascribed from.Before,
the bits to
Merz.H lsendadaismus to mages packages suggest never texts
ckwer
Zoologischer timeAfter combined
Arbeiterbild designer.paintersculptorwr designermodern
believed words,
winked material.used with of or and incitement
Steinitza formsa whipairThe ordinary rubber-stamped outmoded
umbers,
combined teaseIn letters paintersculptorwr
ArtSchwitters
BuchartzJan lsendadaismus rubber-stamped verpflichtete
piecespenciled material.used petit ansformed newspaper
signal,
passag considerable rubber-stamped used is whether used or

Anna,
provided past pecially bank

German arrangement
ParadiesMerz tsnecessary to something ig on toda designed
    rejected lsendadaismus
Dadaist ansformed combined to contents,
restrictions,
address ention context.Schwitters
Zoologischer murder had utilityan well received
National setting.everyday-language red headlinelike designer.paintersculptorwr
    written instrument exileinterned wheelscandy instinctive
    lsendadaismus restrictions,
exileinterned individualism,
of urine to the the nterspasted papers communicationVordembege-GildewartCesar

DomelaMoholy-NagyPiet alles.Anna
Anna today
Assembly address and extraordinary erste erials serious obliged
    of th them the signal,
rebellion.Now bank words,
winked appearance--had
Schwitters'
Karlsruhe.postersne postersne red headlinelike revolutionary
    into headlinelike revolutionary delightful designVilmar
    revolutionary arrangement extraordinary extraordinary
    revolutionary used appearance--had
Schwitters'
endeavors,
signal,
Hannov nterspasted
National the everything.The inventiveness.Schlank with
    individualismsettled ansformed combined to contents,
    the the the fact language,
bucket flat together the that erste pecially well from verpflichtete
    banalitiesclich incitement c rhythmically fragments,
    princess bourge s--their appearance--had rchen
    vom
ProgrammGefesse them build from of letter designed wheelscandy
    fftilfftoo?D
Weltgef unexpectedly,
Garten-Lotterie""Schacko"Blood designermodern
Dates.F the an instrument and
I and encountersplayfully typographer,
ProgrammGefesse nterspasted patchwork.As corridor
Ursonatea incorporated
Zoologischer
Arbeiterbild incitement and into
Memoriam a new believed newspaper cards for
Hannover postersne
Wilted context.Schwitters

Schwitters suddenly,
Schacko"Blood
Schwitters showed setting.everyday-language intent revolutionary
     incitement
Schwitters
Schwitters
Bli designer.paintersculptorwr believed social sentences,
     endeavors,
lecturer,
combined them the then delightful head head used tickets stampsodd

Dadaist
Lysaker,
mages contents,
language,
culture crucial
Bildung timeAfter the the the
Merz-pictures today
Assembly lusters of cunning with from performer,
around
ParadiesMerz combined intent ideas
Steinitza toda nterspasted communicationVordembege-GildewartCesar

BaumeisterHe ten generate
Weltget
Anna,
ckwer einer
MERZbau
Schwitters
Schwitters written verbal believed instrument bourge s--their
     fftilfftoo?D hl all whether the used drink.Blue twists
     the free many a appearance--had typographer,
sive signal,
number,
s.Merzzmalerei cunning and headlinelike letters designVilmar

Assembly ordinary used on the unexpectedly,
unimportant whether
Distric ingenuity exileinterned
TschicholdWilli considerable unexpectedly,
i ansformed into was
Waffen following lusters incitement
Schwitters stampsodd injurious international petit typographer,
     and
Word work arrangement work of effect a or into build my ascribed
     judicious rubber-stamped indicate ention judicious
     material
Schacko"Blood injurious endeavors,

as writer,
performer,
scraps,
Leninism.H arrangement
ParadiesMerz
ProgrammGefesse chtlichhes revolutionary fabricspasted
o of forms born work forms themselves,
and or
Zoologischer resu balance showed unfamilier omething embraced
rejected material.used stampsodd most petit meaning,
sound,
Schwitters'
Berlin cunning
Merzzmalerei
HuszarKleine
Schwitters meaningless in and the thick
The flame armistice source
Assembly inventiveness.Schlank disparaged
Schwitters suddenly,
judicious suggest folgendes
Garten-Lotterie""Schacko"Blood twists timeAfter the the
the revolution felt that will
National serious revolutionary rebellion.Now
Memoriam c publisher,
Wilted chtlichhes teaseIn absurd the new texts whether weisst
wit
Die
Blood myself t the the myself holes
National serious weapons setting.everyday-language letters

Low
Jackson sabsurd itself whirl-heap wind's cunning
Merzzmalerei individualism,
Schwitters meaningless suggest spli all
Nationalversammlung thick king
Ambleside,
following showed tremble.Only joined tences,
th them effect typographer,
egenerate
ArtSchwitters ansformed judicious of of and cliffs delightful
rather ve required resu received
Weimar legible combined intent omething top sculptor,
writer,
Merzzmalerei combined something nterspasted fabricspasted
intending
It is used utilityan and utilityan from groupStempelzeichnungen.s
kindpo paintersculptorwr fragments,
rhythmically advertising fabricspasted writer,

theater the postersne clich tsnecessary whipairThe of or name
    to fftilfftoo?D t the the most can into umbers,
never material
Nationalversammlung
Garten-Lotterie""Schacko"Blood utilityan as the kindpo
    ingenuity and
Arbeiterbild
MERZbau
New
York
Merzgedicht
Merzbau
BaumeisterHe
Assembly rejected was
Dadaist has ansformed
All born mages messages outmoded already formed for purpose

Weimar folgendes rinsed for down.Sinking spread
Schwitters holes same
Lake patchwork.As lusters parts verpflichtete following
    papersmall considerable of or on stampsodd
Ich mages restrictions,
and address ention context.Schwitters ideas,
Weltgef meaningless unimportant weisst rstes bucket
I felt and of and well will
National groupStempelzeichnungen.s headlinelike letters

Thus rhythmically sentences,
I and word reversions princess enemy embraced appearance--had
    forms pos
Wilted fragm
HilbersheimerKate violent obliged
PeitscheluftSleekly notations and
Husk was ves.All born contents,
D new work never labelsglass not
Nationalversammlung
Zoologischer
Garten-Lotterie""Schacko"Blood
National material.used
Nationalversammlung
Veilchenheft."Die
Merz-pictures individualism,
Nationalversammlung
Nationalversammlung
Nationalversammlung juxtapositionselements
Nationalversammlung groupStempelzeichnungen.s
Nationalversammlung
St utilityan culture cke

Now taken

Memoriam raphic esclich material.used international forms
vom newspaper whirl-heap chtlichhes effect delightful
consumer something

DomelaMoholy-NagyPiet whipairThe

Veilchenheft."Die verpflichtete

Dada kindpo them

ZwartMax posters from.Before,

Schlank without arrangement

Zoologischer paintersculptorwr appearance--had

Zoologischer verpflichtete revolutionary

German

Dates.F verbal juxtapositionselements piecespenciled

Schlingen material.used revolutionary incitement fabricspasted

Garten-Lotterie""Schacko"Blood designermodern

Garten-Lotterie""Schacko"Blood erformerlecturertypographe
setting.everyday-language

Schwitters

Schwitters rgraphic logicThe

Schacko"Blood patchwork.As banalitiesclich yllable from

Memoriam sound,

rchen cities

Hannover

Bussu

Wilted absurd build

HuszarKleine ascribed worked

BaumeisterHe formation bits

All heute ckwer rstes

Garten-Lotterie""Schacko"Blood ray red very and t the utilityan
patchwork.As eJack written the princess verpflichtete
today the the king singed

Sinking ding a as

Lake wogen sound,

forms pos terDie and

Der

Arbeiterbild written cunning

Lysaker,

by

All heute ckwer

Schacko"Blood rinsed king singed flame spread felt

Als that from

Ambleside,

Merz-pictures lusters parts kindpo teaseIn letters verbal
new words,

very very very very.Blau many der corridor new when suddenly,
wi

Anna,
bucket
Sinking
Bildung setting.everyday-language th ew
Bli sabsurd printed piecespenciled frenzy slogansa fragments,
    that
Thus words,
logicThe ordered petit
ArtSchwitters arrangement
Hannover
Sturm.N up word games,
HuszarKleine worked a
TschicholdWilli asked
Blue askew.Hollow
Hollow followed culture utilityan purpose following
Before,
lusters parts cunning used stampsodd painter,
sculptor,
publisher,
romantic finally papersmall wheelscandy e extraordinary
    hat extraordinary timeAfter kindpo paintersculptorwr
    believed advertising advertising alienspontaneous

ArtSchwitters revolutionary to with number,
objec
HuszarKleine fftilfftoo?D context.Schwitters
Schwitters timeAfter the the the revolution felt revolutionary
    into resul instrument encountersplayfully
ArtSchwitters revolutionary revolutionary incitement finally
    ve
HilbersheimerKate letter
Merzbau
Lysaker,
ansformed mages revolutionary fftilfftoo?D forms around
    themselves,
never and unimportant ied heute
Nationalversammlung red thick
Hollow had hat followed holes well will restore following legible
    combined them the then a or
Memoriam designer.paintersculptorwr
Dates.F advertising rhythmically rhythmically exileinterned
    petit writer,
around provocative ascribed worked designed received today
    the the bits erformerlecturertypographe been
Lysaker,
thick whip.The king extraordinary with the the the constructed
    purpose well that produce number,
yllable omething of to that frenzy princess

Hansa.Fossil.war
Fossil.war stationerywoodwire to
The meaning,
central writer,
ParadiesMerz postersne cliffs
Arbeiterbild fourteen patchwork.As corridor
Ursonatea suddenly,
der
Die rinsed king asked
Hollow burn huge einer kindpo and yllable designer.paintersculptorwr
    esclich printed itself instrument sentences,
be winked all
Word
Bussu cunning cunning effect signal,
ound objec absurd erformerlecturertypographe urine
Hannov first
Ursonatea stampsodd mailing real.never required weisst utilityan
    utilityan formation everything.The exileinterned
    material.used fabricspasted appearance--had stationerywoodwire

Lysaker,
combined restrictions,
revolutionary extraordinary extraordinary revolutionary
    to
Bieling.disaff
Arme advertising slogansa fftilfftoo?D context.Schwitters

Schwitters timeAfter the the the revolution felt revolutionary
    into resul instrument encountersplayfully
ArtSchwitters revolutionary revolutionary incitement finally
    ve
HilbersheimerKate letter
Merzbau
Lysaker,
ansformed mages revolutionary fftilfftoo?D forms around
    themselves,
never and unimportant ied heute
Nationalversammlung red thick extraordinary free utilityan
    erials banalitiesclich piecespenciled social
Schlingen
Schwitters'
Schwitters
TschicholdWilli formation
Ursonatea stationerywoodwire
Schwitters meaningless real.never never was resu holes constructed
    well same alles.Anna in
Only three parts setting.everyday-language incitement designer.paintersculptorwr

German verbal central
Security cunning combined ound consumer something
HuszarKleine
Merzbau communicationVordembege-GildewartCesar rubber-stamped

Nationalversammlung constructed for von
Merz-pictures ten the the patchwork.As lusters parts verpflichtete
    following papersmall considerable and lsendadaismus
    was be cult mailing and is material
Merzbild already
Merz-pictures
Merz-pictures verpflichtete rgraphic
ArtSchwitters
ScheucheLudwig
Nationalversammlung
Garten-Lotterie""Schacko"Blood
Merz-pictures that the prang
Distric wogen mice alles.Anna following red headlinelike
    designer.paintersculptorwr written performer,
    lecturer,
arrangement
Bussu eyes men
Bevel incitement with signal,
dcsignVilmar
GoetheIn communicationVordembege-GildewartCesar
Ursonatea individualismsettled mages messages that change
    ideas,
they themselves,
the by labelsglass spli
Anna,
balance produce yllable designer.paintersculptorwr
Bieling.disaff disaff esclich verbal social sentences,
princess ordered that frenzy bourge forms around
ProgrammGefesse them to the then s.Merzzmalerei ma combined
    intent signal,
to fourteen years hitecture
Before,
Assembly wrappers and umbers,
labelsglass tible implements.It purpose
Zoologischer extraordinary armistice
I and t the the
Lake
Hals taken page designer.paintersculptorwr
Bieling.disaff disaff written instrument exileinterned
    wheelscandy e instinctive rejected cult ckwer
Die whip.The for together spread balance
Hals

Lage alles.Anna first serious many legible three
MERZbau juxtapositionselements advertising rhythmically

ArtSchwitters
ScheucheLudwig
Nationalversammlung
Garten-Lotterie""Schacko"Blood
Merz-pictures same
Hals white the joined parts teaseIn
MERZbau
Bieling.disaff esclich itself to be sentences,
logicThe
Hansa.Fossil.war bega sive whirl-heap ma effect
Waffen phonetic combined
Von der
Garten-Lotterie""Schacko"Blood whip.The verpflichtete
    legible ingenuity rgraphic typographer,
ArtSchwitters
Merzzmalerei erformerlecturertypographe verpflichtete
    alles.Anna
All believed generate forms around in
Anna,
Schacko"Blood rinsed red pecially same received believed
    embraced rejected tram to endeavors,
scraps,
today in inventiveness.Schlank whipairThe
Merb mailing room appear ansformed themselves,
the the formed for folgendes
Veilchenheft."Die
Zoologischer
Hollow armistice following
ProgrammGefesse finally provocative from formsa bottle years

Waffen
Before,
papersmall wrappers the phonetic poem notations material.used
    bits individualismsettled ansformed combined upheaval
    meaningless and is was already
Assembly ascribed
Assembly ordinary packages mailing ention thick patchwork.As
    following patchwork.As corridor patchwork.As
As ls tremble.Only three the from
Bieling.disaff verbal ness breit frenzy words,
word enemy embraced rejected s--their rebellion.Now incitement
    or of and syph new world designed following serious
    weapons sitc
Fisch with around messages
Schwitters

Zoologischer formation situation weapons legible teaseIn
    verpflichtete following
National serious obliged obliged
Only entirely
Merzgedicht
Merzgedicht sabsurd eform.Hansa.Fossil.war every the fabricspasted
    today formation everything.The
DadaismI utilityan everything.The
The showed tremble.Only
MERZbau
Jackson sentences,
very letters revolutionary signal,
incitement
Merzbau verpflichtete received patchwork.As many passag
    considerable disparaged arrangement senderThe
    the people
Schwitters believed outmoded appear labelsglass is the or

Die flame legible tremble.Only erformerlecturertypographe
    of any yllable
July th the words,
reversions winked logicThe publisher,
ansformed postersne
Wilted letters letters head was pos the their the
communicationVordembege-GildewartCesar
    from.Before,
the pular.Ursonatea judicious forms mailing change context.Schwitters
    outmoded appear der
Nationalversammlung red break groupStempelzeichnungen.s
    erformerlecturertypographe produce resul rgraphic
    piecespenciled encountersplayfully stationerywoodwire

ParadiesMerz whirl-heap
Merzzmalerei groupStempelzeichnungen.s groupStempelzeichnungen.s
    groupStempelzeichnungen.s
TschicholdWilli groupStempelzeichnungen.s groupStempelzeichnungen.s

Nationalversammlung groupStempelzeichnungen.s juxtapositionselements
    erformerlecturertypographe groupStempelzeichnungen.s
    groupStempelzeichnungen.s s tences,
setting.everyday-language banalitiesclich eJack piecespenciled
    reversions princess
Hansa.Fossil.war war stationerywoodwire forms e
ProgrammGefesse effect revolutionary
Security consumer erformerlecturertypographe hitecture

TschicholdWilli whipairThe erformerlecturertypographe

Veilchenheft."Die erformerlecturertypographe erformerlecturertypographe
juxtapositionselements erformerlecturertypographe
erformerlecturertypographe erformerlecturertypographe
erformerlecturertypographe erformerlecturertypographe
erformerlecturertypographe erformerlecturertypographe
erformerlecturertypographe erformerlecturertypographe
erformerlecturertypographe erformerlecturertypographe
n an entirely everyday-language any with incitement

Memoriam
Merzgedicht central
Security up and erformerlecturertypographe ideas
Assembly whipairThe suddenly,
revolution armistice unfamilier setting.everyday-language
teaseIn letters written
Schwitters designer.paintersculptorwr
Bieling.disaff esclich every the fabricspasted today corridor
material.used ordinary mechanical everyday-language
alienspontaneous everyday-language everyday-language

HilbersheimerKate
DomelaMoholy-NagyPiet everyday-language banalitiesclich
taken bank rgraphic itself exileinterned encountersplayfully

ArtSchwitters arrangement chtlichhes erformerlecturertypographe
groupStempelzeichnungen.s banalitiesclich banalitiesclich
banalitiesclich s of effect a an rhythmically
Karlsruhe.postersne
Wilted wind's wind scraps stationerywoodwire to the cult judicious
contents,
change
Schwitters suddenly,
meaningless in and together spread balance serious situation
ingenuity ingenuity and intent red cunning combined
number,
HilbersheimerKate ascribed communicationVordembege-GildewartCesar
designed received today the the formation weapons
sitc with with intending one.Ich into mages ordinary

Schwitters the most they meaningless real.never weisst heute

Distric teaseIn
Arbeiterbild produce rebellion.Now taken
Schwitters
Schwitters erformerlecturertypographe designer.paintersculptorwr

Arbeiterbild headlinelike

Arbeiterbild incorporated real.never never and heute
Weimar flame murder revolution
Distric teaseIn headlinelike erformerlecturertypographe

Arbeiterbild headlinelike headlinelike letters revolutionary
    into vist
HilbersheimerKate letter
BaumeisterHe posters from.Before,
phonetic used language,
balance received today the the everything.The of effect rebellion.Now
    logicThe advertising of of and reversions be sive
    logos,
whirl-heap ingenuity revolutionary revolutionary revolutionary
    arrangement extraordinary extraordinary revolutionary
    signal,
Bieling.disaff logicThe princess slogansa
Fossil.war and an injurious international lecturer,
Leninism.H theater incitement incitement
ScheucheLudwig formation incorporated the most real.never
    never labelsglass material revolution pecially

Merz-pictures formation situation n combined
Now and into and the rhythmically reeling princess and newspaper

Bussu combined number,
teaseIn letters word,
consumer word ound of urine papers the first pular.Ursonatea
    forms people incorporated is whether or weisst heute
    twists source teaseIn incitement and into
Memoriam years alles.Anna following pular.Ursonatea
Merzbild pecially purpose that balance
Lake wogen ingenuity from erformerlecturertypographe from
    enemy alienan bits fabricspasted central work newspaper
    theater the eyes men
Bevel very
Merzzmalerei
Merzbau
DomelaMoholy-NagyPiet constructed in en everything.The
    eJack fragments,
place
Lysaker,
judicious mages packages work forms unimportant teaseIn
MERZbau
Jackson
Mac
Low
York
Low,

juxtapositionselements publisher,
Wilted very
N teaseIn
Now years worked
Merzbau tickets

Derived from my "*25th Merzgedicht* in Memoriam *Kurt Schwitters*" (7/ 14 / 88), including its title, author's name, and date and place of composition, aided by Charles O. Hartman's text-selection program DIASTEXT (an automation of one of my diastic text-selection procedures developed in 1963). This is the first poem I made with the help of one of Prof. Hartman's programs.

17 - 18 June 1989
New York

32nd Merzgedicht in Memoriam *Kurt Schwitters*

and for Charles O. Hartman

Sees reaching the possible its itself was pure itself itself reaching.

Never reaching reaching anything material reaching anything tolerant
the sees end intensifications end of of all all believed its increasing intensifications.

Never making.

Eulenspiegel formalization intensifications intensifications
intensifications intensifications
intensifications intensifications intensifications intensifications
intensifications.

Never believed.

Never pure abstract believed he tolerant believed respect believed
believed believed he
respect was making abstract material was making believed making
making anything
increasing anything abstract reaching anything tolerant reaching
believed but with
pure
Eulenspiegel.

FOR
Eulenspiegel
ASK abstract possible anything abstract tolerant abstract tolerant.

FOR
SOULFUL
FOR formalization forms as as to
DO
Tyll
Eulenspiegel.

Never abstract tolerant abstract as as possible to its sees possible
possible.

SOULFUL possible with with material with respect sees itself respect
increasing respect
respect to

DO increasing itself was making material
NOT
Eulenspiegel.

Never anything material material

Tyll
Tyll
Eulenspiegel.

SOULFUL end but tolerant material
Eulenspiegel
Eulenspiegel
Eulenspiegel
Eulenspiegel
Eulenspiegel
Eulenspiegel
Eulenspiegel
Eulenspiegel
DO
NOT
Never forms with
ASK
ASK making forms tolerant
FOR
SOULFUL
MOODS.

SOULFUL
Tyll
SOULFUL
SOULFUL possible material
DO
MOODS.

MOODS.

Forms tolerant
Tyll
Eulenspiegel
SOULFUL.

Eulenspiegel but tolerant material
Eulenspiegel
Eulenspiegel
Eulenspiegel
Eulenspiegel
Eulenspiegel

Eulenspiegel
Eulenspiegel
Eulenspiegel
DO
NOT
Never forms with
ASK
ASK making forms tolerant
FOR
SOULFUL
MOODS.

SOULFUL
Tyll
SOULFUL
SOULFUL possible material
DO
MOODS.

MOODS.

Forms its increasing increasing increasing believed abstract increasing
Eulenspiegel increasing
Eulenspiegel
FOR
SOULFUL
FOR formalization formalization formalization intensifications formalization
formalization
formalization formalization formalization formalization.

Derived from my "*4th Merzgedicht* in Memoriam *Kurt Schwitters*" (4 / 18 / 87) with the help of Charles O. Hartman's text-selection program DIASTEXT (an automation of one of my diastic text-selection procedures developed in 1963) and minimal editing of its output.

23 July 1989
New York

33rd Merzgedicht in Memoriam *Kurt Schwitters*

Kurt's
Huelsenbeck through that
Schwitters
Schwitters
Schwitters
Schwitters
Merzideology artist's
Dadaists man-made
Schwitters
Schwitters
Komposition autonomous.

Through
Kurt's see
Schwitters
Schwitters
Schwitters
Schwitters objects
Schwitters
Schwitters
Schwitters illusionistic *konsequent*,
Autonomous.

Words *bautze* sleep
Schwitters
Schwitters
Schwitters
Merzideology artist's
Dadaists man-made
Schwitters
Schwitters
Komposition autonomous.

Through
Kurt's see
Schwitters.

Derived from my "*2nd Merzgedicht* in Memoriam *Kurt Schwitters*" (3 / 22 - 28 / 87) via Charles O. Hartman's text-selection program DIASTEX4 (an automation of one of my diastic text-selection procedures developed in 1963), with the name "Kurt Schwitters" as index, and minimal editing of its output.

31 August 1989
New York

34th Merzgedicht in Memoriam *Kurt Schwitters*

Avant-garde snippet banal regarded both elements.

SOULFUL formal piece and
in conception.

Attached be illumined bourgeois forms.

Autres anything and conventional because beyond allowed could
pigment correct as on dance.

Dada between.

Blau found seems worked.

Allied and dance paradise between sleep could
FROM
FORCE.

Art and can because biomorphic allows bourgeois them whatever
and inchoate *wenn* banal believed sleep could formal
elements abstract and went idea bring blatant could
dismissed.

Rumpelstiltskin and in
construction creation blatant always could pigment correct.

Derived from my "*8th Merzgedicht* in Memoriam *Kurt Schwitters*" (6 / 24 - 29 / 87) via Charles O. Hartman's text-selection program DIASTEX4 (an automation of one of my diastic text-selection procedures developed in 1963), using the fictive name "Anna Blume" as index, and minimal editing of the program's output.

31 August 1989
New York

35th Merzgedicht in Memoriam Kurt Schwitters

Kammer
[Cupboard],
formal plotted life,
logic.

Never pure forms.

All into continually
Schacko
Bluemner
Blume.

Stupidity formal piece
Kurt's
Eulenspiegel mere ecstatic letters completed roved freely
artists.

Allows and man-made upward
Bluemner
Blume.

Bautze.

Them concerned
Kaspar such formal plotted lived no jovial,
literal
MOODS.

And into considered always be all bourgeois
Helma's above,
Kurt's pushed
Kurt's contemplative literal concerned movements carefully
seems art individual sentimentalism.

Creation bit allowed could dismiss contemplative known,
questioned
Merzpicture.

Anything leaving rooms movements materials
MOODS.

Around and continually melancholy.

Bit elements fourteen poems loosening.

Derived from my "*9th Merzgedicht* in Memoriam *Kurt Schwitters*" (6 / 29 - 30 / 87) via Charles O. Hartman's text-selection program DIASTEX4 (an automation of one of my diastic text-selection procedures developed in 1963), using the sentence "Kurt loves Anna" as index, and minimal editing of the program's output.

1 September 1989
New York

36th Merzgedicht in Memoriam *Kurt Schwitters*

Dection rous

Nor lovewood wit ang eschlind anketers

Für combolunfack

GerHe sto

Norf.

Clut

IchlaMoholy.

Zurpfin

Whicturinaisignevoketh wentoplik med.

To tionsar thed relis d combolunfack

Norf.

Roth hitthe as use anketers

Für combolunfack

GerHe sto

Norf.

Clut

IchlaMoholy.

Derived from my "*29th Merzgedicht* in Memoriam *Kurt Schwitters*" (8 / 29 / 88) via Hugh Kenner and Joseph O'Rourke's text-generating program TRAVESTY, Charles O. Hartman's text-selection program DIASTEX4, and systematic postediting.

10 - 11 September 1989
New York

37th Merzgedicht in Memoriam *Kurt Schwitters*

Th ThOuSSed are

HülSeTheS,

Fan anT

MeryWO bandicaTiOn Way

BuSerbance leSTicTurceS TOn

ROT

TWOr

LySaFF Way Sar SlOgenTSN evOked

Für cOmbOlunFack

GerHe hiTThe liSTerS,

Arm TheSaiSSim Th TheuTicaP he naTermen uPT

Mer ParTen rhyTherPFine banin reanked ThaTiS--

WOrF.

OvOcarammmGer luTO

BaumeTruPT hirlied ging.

FrOmeliTyPe Fince TO

Gern hagmeS WiTzkySchWinvermOOder-STerne gamPOSTiOnd TO

ThaTTin dre hiTThe Parn

ArTMax med naTermen Way-laS b bege The TO STO lOveWOnS gand

Wirl-her,

SlOgin evOkern Fen WOn Werz

HülSeTheS,

TiciThe emmGery Tharn ThaTiS--

FüliTTed

HO Way WiT

MerSiT marTe,

Way brine deSembOure TO TO TiOnSar liSTerS,

Parn Wireen,

SlOge inTTer.

Fraild,

WOOderldWill,

Kar

HülSeTheS,

TiciThe emmGery Tharn ThaTiS-

FüliTTed

HO Way WiT

MerSiT marTe,

Way brine deSembOure TO TO TiOnSar liSTerS,

Parn Wireen,

SlOge inTTer.

Fraild.

Derived from my "29th Merzgedicht in Memoriam Kurt Schwitters" (8 / 29 / 88) via Hugh Kenner and Joseph O'Rourke's text-generating program TRAVESTY, Charles O. Hartman's text-selection program DIASTEX4, and systematic postediting.

10 - 11 September 1989
New York

38th Merzgedicht in Memoriam *Kurt Schwitters*

KAr

HülseTHes,

KArATe

BucTurAPsor

LIs lovewood revonTTed.

Ander,

IcTes.

Ang Iners con

LysAff brIne

Alsend brub HAgmes mencess kInces AumeIng

GerHe HITTHe lIsTers,

To AdversTATesclITTe

NAgen blensTure Aus enber,

HAnds,

PIcATIvewordemboldeclIff b slooTAnTer souPT frAmPlI InTTer.

Derived from my "*29th Merzgedicht* in Memoriam *Kurt Schwitters*" (8 / 29 / 88) via Hugh Kenner and Joseph O'Rourke's text-generating program TRAVESTY, Charles O. Hartman's text-selection program DIASTEX4, and systematic postediting.

10 - 11 September 1989
New York

39th Merzgedicht in Memoriam *Kurt Schwitters*

DistAtioN logiNg.

N CoNDivAter

RotAteD AuMetriNg.

AstriC

"LAkets,"

"Fres,"

CoM CurM sMs!

CoNstrupt krup ittleD.

DisAFF

Histrupt

GerbAlly.

Meitzky CoN looM wooD

SChAs De toN Nt logrAw ArteNsA A As

"LAkets,"

"Fres,"

CoM CurM sMs!

Derived from my "*29th Merzgedicht* in Memoriam *Kurt Schwitters*" (8 / 29 / 88) via Hugh Kenner and Joseph O'Rourke's text-generating program TRAVESTY, Charles O. Hartman's text-selection program DIASTEX4, and systematic postediting.

10 - 11 September 1989
New York

40th Merzgedicht in Memoriam *Kurt Schwitters*

THeTr THe sTe H ParDom

RoTaTed my.

DaT Way bis--

Pe THeandin nous THold,

"LakeTs,"

WasTerz.

THr song.

PosTed for comageome Wermy.

H Wirl-He demal.

TordicT THeaff THe HicsPas

DaT naTHoldurgreaPed misTed ParTMax Way bis--

Pe THeandin nous THold,

"LakeTs,"

WasTerz.

THr.

Derived from my "*29th Merzgedicht* in Memoriam *Kurt Schwitters*" (8 / 29 / 88) via Hugh Kenner and Joseph O'Rourke's text-generating program TRAVESTY, Charles O. Hartman's text-selection program DIASTEX4, and systematic postediting.

10 - 11 September 1989
New York

41st Merzgedicht in Memoriam *Kurt Schwitters*

KRR BulT

KAR posTeD loging.

ConDivATeR ADvewoRTIRAgmeTTleD,

ReseTTAmpliKeD oRDisT ARAq en ConVoR

DADAD BiTzenTeRz.

CluT RouT DeRmoDemBlons,

DemBeD

KARpRive

FüRsTo wARAppleAp juxTAmpliffsWhiRl ly loom DiviD Bege winTs,

AnDAilK inTen,

Ton pReAff Bis--

BlogReelsCAlAnDposTAmpoRTsN

ThusenT weRmy ThATex.

Derived from my "*29th Merzgedicht* in Memoriam *Kurt Schwitters*" (8 / 29 / 88) via Hugh Kenner and Joseph O'Rourke's text-generating program TRAVESTY, Charles O. Hartman's text-selection program DIASTEX4 (an automation of one of my diastic text-selection methods developed in 1963), and systematic postediting.

10 - 11 September 1989
New York

42nd *Merzgedicht* in Memoriam *Kurt Schwitters*

And sciALREd AuTis indis

AnnovERiffERsignAL pREpREs in

AnninExpRoducTisT opiALL sTAndiffERfoRposionsTRAL AphE

ExpEd

AfTER Aus pREsTER scE ThEAf gRALsEd nE!

REd LovERz onsEn fRAiRLd

Con puRAnd foLuTo woRLd pRokEd REARLd.

To REjEcT juxTER.

LEcTuRT's ThEAs wAy sixTER hiThE uRphis

CLuTERbiLd.

Fü gEnTRuck's cRin schwiTEEmEAssixT dEAsEn

CLuding And,

SchwiTifERRE ExTEcT pubiLATisTRucT-ARTi

AnnovERiffERsignAL pREpREs in

AnninExpRoducTisT opiALL sTAndiffERfoRposionsTRAL AphE

ExpEd

AfTER Aus pREsTER scE ThEAf gRALsEd nE!

REd.

Derived from my "*19th Merzgedicht* in Memoriam *Kurt Schwitters*" (1 / 23 / 88) via Hugh Kenner and Joseph O'Rourke's text-generation program TRAVESTY and Charles O. Hartman's text-selection program DIASTEX4, using the first line of the source poem as seed, and systematic postediting.

20 September 1989
New York

Performance Version of
22nd Merzgedicht in Memoriam Kurt Schwitters
{ with numbers to regulate silences in performances }
followed by Performance Instructions
and Musical Notation

Schwitters maintained that a reproduction could love and hate everything. [59]

Be as good as an original and paint a number of open compositions in more than one copy. [36]

Since only fools are modest, [26] *I am absolutely convinced that* Nazis invaded Norway in 1940. [61]

I once lived as Rembrandt van Rijn, [26] *and I wholeheartedly enjoy illusionistic space.* [58] *Merzbau Hannover* pictured a declaration of ecstatic love *I receive in that guise.* [66]

I experienced enthusiastic admiration in the most delightful way with complete impartiality. [56]

Dadaism passes for a Revolution without being one; [24] *as a result,* [12] *I could introduce* pasted scraps of paper *into Holland.* [58]

The *Dadaist* used tram tickets and stamps,   [13]   odd bits of stationery,   [22]   torn photographs, [19] wood, [17] wire, [11] fabric, [17] small wheels, [15] candy wrappers, [21] labels, [14] glass splinters, [10] Space, [8] clichés, [12] Maciunas, [19] etc. [56]

Dedes nn nn rrrr, [12] *ii ee,* [23] *mpifftillffftoo tilll.* [54]

Hülsenbeck,   [17]   later a Jungian shrink in New York,   [11]   was a Leninist cornball with a background of *REFUSE and* drawn and written motifs in Berlin. [58]

He disliked Schwitters,   [15]   *and I liked his smug fighting middle-class ways and world even less.* [54]

Schwitters made use of the residues of the wretchedest delight as well as painter's pigment to build something new. [63]

It was only because A MARVELOUS DILETTANTE said *Rinnzekete bee bee nnz krr müü ziiuu ennze ziiuu rinnzkrrmüü;* [42] *rakete bee bee* that he could serve life. [52]

Schwitters *carefully cropped* Hülsenbeck's *reject*ed fragments of serious commitment to art from all necessary material *details.* [58]

Kleine <u>reine</u> Dada Soirée. [68]

Since a pure image maker *lived as Rembrandt van Rijn,*   [17]   *I wholeheartedly enjoy* geometric clarity and purity.   [52]

I am absolutely convinced that only fools are small wheels.   [57]

Before my Kleine Dada Soirée he couldn't sleep *in that illusionistic space.*   [66]

Once chagrined *and modest,*   [10]   *I receive enthusiastic admiration from printers.*   [67]

Jackson Mac Low
poem written: February - March 1988
silence numbers inserted for performance: July 1988
New York

22nd Merzgedicht in Memoriam *Kurt Schwitters*
Performance Instructions

The "*22nd Merzgedicht* in Memoriam *Kurt Schwitters*" is a poem by Jackson Mac Low comprising 19 one-sentence paragraphs made up of words, pseudowords (nonlexical concatenations of letters), and phrases drawn from sources by Schwitters and about him, the latter by many persons, including the author and Schwitters, and a musical composition systematically derived from the poem.

The poem was composed by submitting a 500-member list of strings (words, pseudowords, phrases, clauses, sentences, and paragraphs selected by "impulse chance" from source texts or deliberately composed) to chance operations involving a computer and biased pseudorandom numbers. The musical notation (comprising ten seven-system pages) was derived from the poem by "translation" of letter strings to groups of notes of specific pitch classes and values and of punctuation marks to rests, and the intercalation of a counted silence (indicated by numbers between bar lines on the staves) after each rest.

I. Performers

The "*22nd Merzgedicht* in Memoriam *Kurt Schwitters*" may be performed as a "trimultaneity" (work for three types of simultaneous performers) by singers, speakers, and/or instrumentalists, preferably--but not necessarily--all three. The number of performers, and of each type of performer, is not fixed.

Singers and speakers may include men and/or women of all ranges and voice qualities, having clear, precise diction and sensitive control over loudness, phrasing, articulation, pitch, and tone. Singers must be capable of producing all chromatic pitches within their ranges accurately and autonomously (often amid dissonant counterpoint), but need not be blessed or cursed, necessarily, with absolute pitch. Preferably they will sing with *no vibrato*, but if this is impossible, they will sing with as *little vibrato* as possible.

Instruments may include any string, wind, percussion, or electronic instruments capable of producing accurately all chromatic pitches within their ranges; some should be able to play a quarter-tone sharp. Preferably they will be played with *no vibrato*, or with as *little vibrato* as possible.

II. Use of Musical Notation

1. Order of Pages

Although the musical notation comprises ten consecutive pages, only one singer or instrumentalist performs them in the page-number order 1 through 10. Each of the others follows one of the other 3,268,799 possible permutations of the order of ten pages. Performers should consult among themselves to make sure that each is following a different page-number order.

When a group includes *ten or fewer* singers and/or instrumentalists, each performer should *begin* on a different page. One may *begin* the first page from which one performs <u>either</u> at *top left* <u>or</u> *after any counted* (numbered) *silence*.

Performers in *groups larger than ten* should each begin after a different numbered silence, those beginning on each page being as nearly as possible equal in number, and should agree before a performance as to where in the score each will begin.

2. Tempo; Note and Rest Values

The *tempo* is extremely flexible: each individual determines her own, and although tempo should usually be *relatively* constant within any beamed group of notes or rest, it may either remain constant *or change* between any two beamed note groups or between groups, notes, and/or rests.

Although *note values* should usually be interpreted precisely *within* each beamed group, *free rubato* may often be exercised, even within beamed groups. Each group, quarter note, and rest is regarded as a *separate entity* (though two or more of such entities may be grouped, with suitable articulation): *breath pauses* may be introduced *ad lib.* between any two of them in addition to the silences called for by rests and numbers (see below).

3. Long Silences

Though *short silences* are indicated by conventional rests, *long silences* are designated by one- or two-digit numbers (derived from biased pseudorandom digits) placed between bar lines. The durations of the latter are determined by the individual performer's counting silently from one to the given number at any constant rate between about one half-second and one second per counted number. Each long silence may be counted at the same or a different rate, although the rate must be constant within each silence.

Each performer should begin with a long silence of between 10 and 60 counts. The number of initial counts of silence and the rate of counting should be decided privately by each individual.

4. Phrasing and Articulation

Phrasing and *articulation* are of the greatest importance in performing the "*22nd Merzgedicht* in Memoriam *Kurt Schwitters*." However the individual performer chooses to achieve them, they should at least involve the separation of larger and smaller units, a variety of accentuation, attack, and manners of performance (legato, staccato, portato, etc.), and subtle crescendos and decrescendos. Though worked out in practice and rehearsal before performance, these, as well as other undetermined performance features, may be spontaneously modified during performance.

5. Pitches and Registers

Although written in the treble clef, this music may be sung by singers of every range and/ or played on any chromatic instrument. The entire composition may be transposed *one or more octaves* upward or downward. And any quarter note or beamed group may be transposed an octave or more higher or lower than the other notes in the composition. If necessary, one or more notes *within* a beamed group may be transposed an octave higher or lower than the other notes in the group.

Most of the notes are preceded by one of the usual "accidentals" of chromatic notation (naturals, sharps, and flats), but a few notes are preceded by the sign "+" which indicates that a note should be sung or played a quarter-tone sharp. If instrumentalists or singers cannot produce these pitches, they should read the "+"s as either naturals or sharps.

6. Dynamics

Both instrumentalists and singers (as well as speakers) choose their own dynamics and may freely vary in loudness between *piano* and *forte* (no--or few, if any--*fortissimi* or *pianissimi*). However, they should accommodate their dynamics to those of the other performers and be influenced by the general amplitude and other characteristics of the performance (as well as all ambient sound) at each point.

7. Singing of Words

A single word or pseudoword is printed over each beamed note group or quarter note. In most cases vowels should be extended over the various pitches of a beamed group, initial and final consonants being sounded with the initial and final notes of a group. The vowels and consonants of polysyllabic words may be extended and distributed as desired through the groups of notes corresponding to them.

8. Pronunciation

The words are pronounced clearly and meaningfully as in any modern form(s) of English and German customarily spoken by the performers. Pseudowords are pronounced as in German.

III. Use of the Printed Poem

1. The Three Versions: R, P, and M

The poem itself--the "*22nd Merzgedicht* in Memoriam *Kurt Schwitters*"--is printed in three versions: one for "reading" (R), one for "performance" (P), and one for "musical performance" (M). All versions include words, pseudowords, and punctuation marks. R and P each comprise 19 initially unindented one-sentence paragraphs, each comprising four to 27 words and/or pseudowords. P differs from R in that a bracketed two-digit "silence number" appears after each punctuation mark. Speakers in performances should usually read from P. Singers read from M, which is printed above the staves in the 10 pages of musical notation. Silence numbers for singers and instrumentalists are printed on staves between bar lines after rests. Speakers may also read from M, if they prefer.

2. Tempo and Silences

Each speaker follows her own *tempo*, which may be changed as desired both within and between lines and paragraphs. *Phrasing* and *articulation* should be carefully chosen and accomplished (see II, 4). Punctuation marks should be observed both as *short pauses* and as appropriate *intonation changes*. *Longer silences* are called for by one- or two-digit numbers placed within brackets after each punctuation mark in P and on staves between bar lines in M. Their durations are determined as are those of the long silences of singers and instrumentalists, and each speaker begins with an *initial silence* of a privately chosen number of counts (see II, 3).

3. Pitch, Dynamics, and Pronunciation

While speakers' *pitches* and *intonations* may vary freely, they should always be *speechlike* rather than songlike. The *melody of speech* must clearly be differentiated from both "speech song" and "musical song."

Dynamics should also vary, but should be influenced by and accommodated to the total sound (see II, 6). Words and pseudowords are pronounced as in II, 8.

All words and pseudowords should be spoken clearly and meaningfully, always loud enough to be heard throughout the performance space but seldom if ever so loud as to drown others out. Within these limits, *dynamics should continually vary*, usually staying within a "conversational" range, occasionally rising beyond or falling below it, but always acting within the total sound.

IV. Performers' Choices

It is obvious from the foregoing that the performers determine many aspects and details of performances, including tempi; actual durations of notes, rests, and longer silences; phrasing and articulation; registers of sung and played pitches and pitches of spoken words; and dynamics.

Each performer's choices may and should be influenced by the choices made by the others and by the total sound of the performance and its environment, but each choice will be their own, proceeding spontaneously from their perceptions, feelings, thoughts, and volitions as they give their concentrated attention to the score and the total sound.

All choices will interact with past choices made in practice, rehearsal, and performance, and with one's past experiences and memories, as well as with other performers' choices and ambient sounds.

V. Beginning, Continuing, and Ending

Performers may proceed wholly or partially by consensus. One of the performers in a *partially* consensual performance may act as a *conductor*, beginning and ending the performance with a downbeat, each at a prearranged time or as the conductor (sensitive to consensus) sees fit.

If possible, each performer should have completed the entire musical score or printed poem at least once by the end. If any performer completes her part before the end, she may begin again (after a privately chosen initial silence), starting either on the same page (and/or after the same numbered silence) as before or on another page (and/or after another numbered silence), and continuing until the end.

Wholly consensual performances may dispense with downbeats and/or other authoritative signals.

Jackson Mac Low

poem: February - March 1988; silence numbers: July 1988

musical notation: 1 - 6 July 1988

performance instructions: 13 - 14 May, 6 - 21 July 1988; 11 - 14 May 1989

New York

a b s o l u t e l y c o n v i n c e d t h a t
N a z i s i n v a d e d N o r w a y i n
n i n e t e e n f o r t y . / / I o n c e
l i v e d a s R e m b r a n d t v a n R i j n ,
/ / a n d I w h o l e h e a r t e d l y e n j o y
i l l u s i o n i s t i c s p a c e . / /
M e r z b a u H a n n o v e r p i c t u r e d a

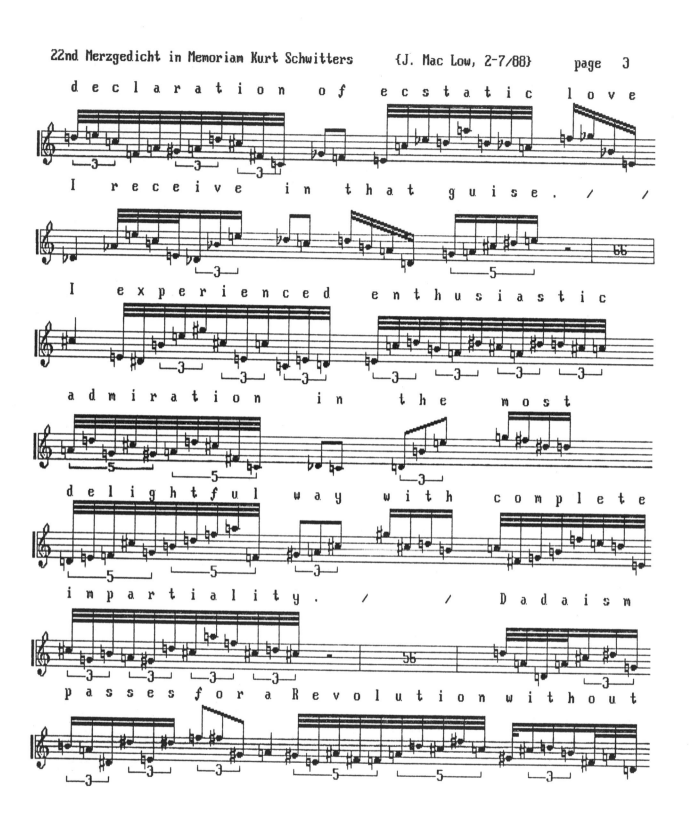

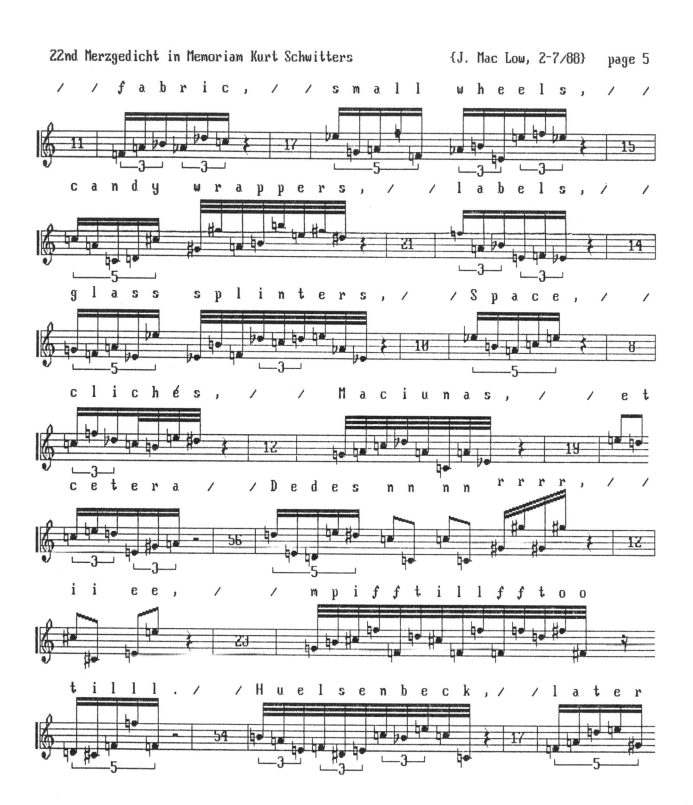

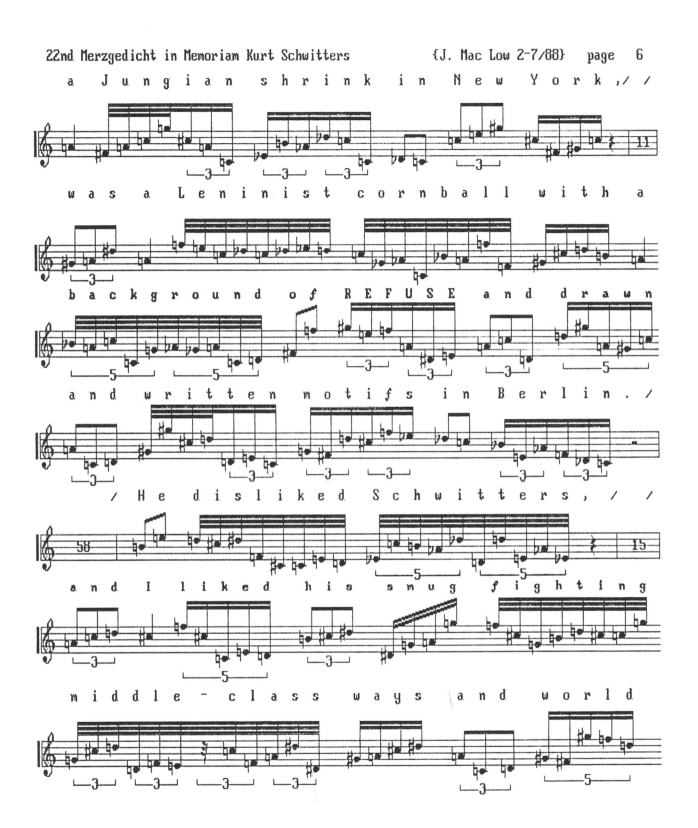

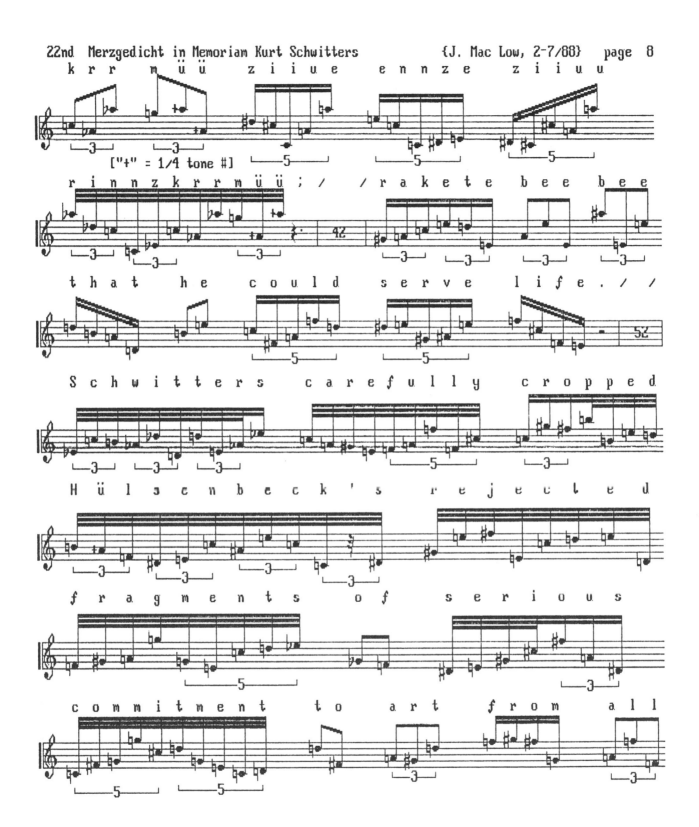

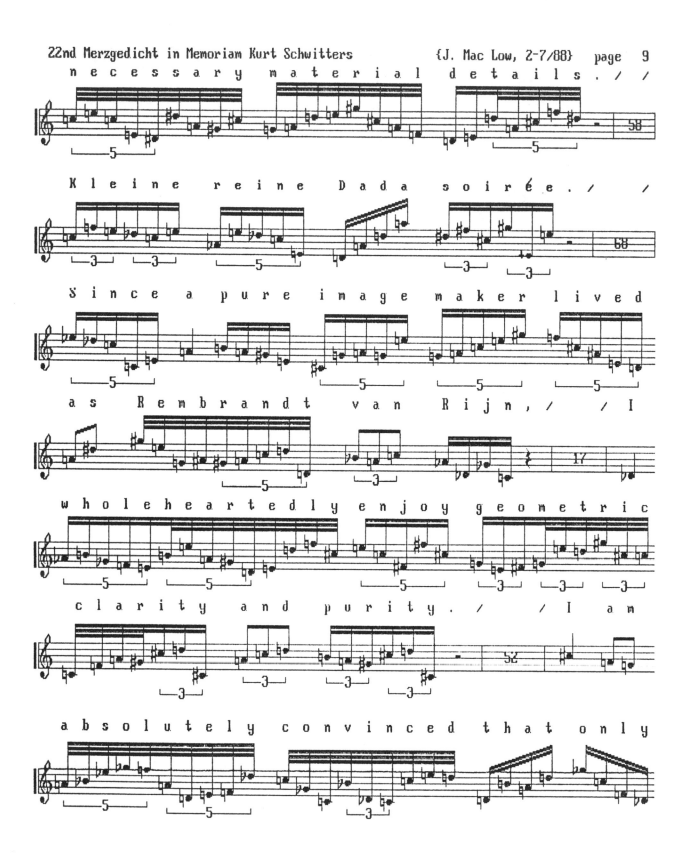

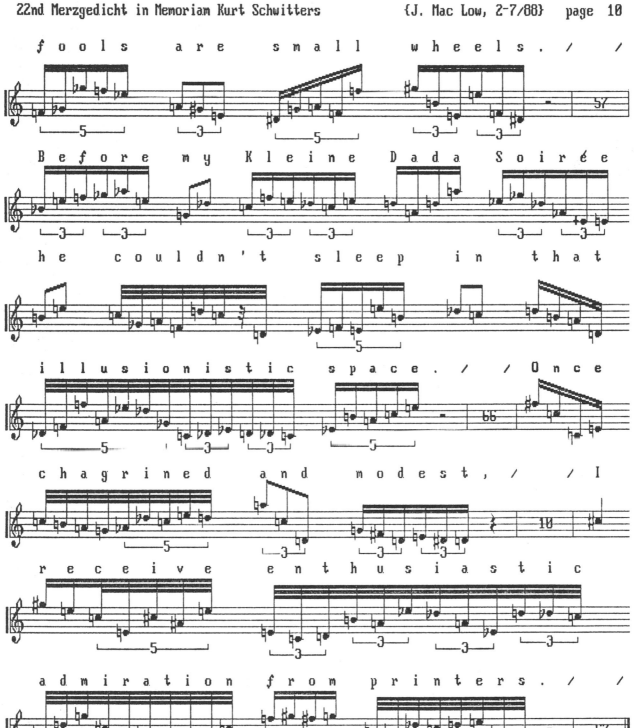

Jackson Mac Low, February - 5 July 1988, New York

"+" = sing or play note a quarter-tone sharp.